I0497649

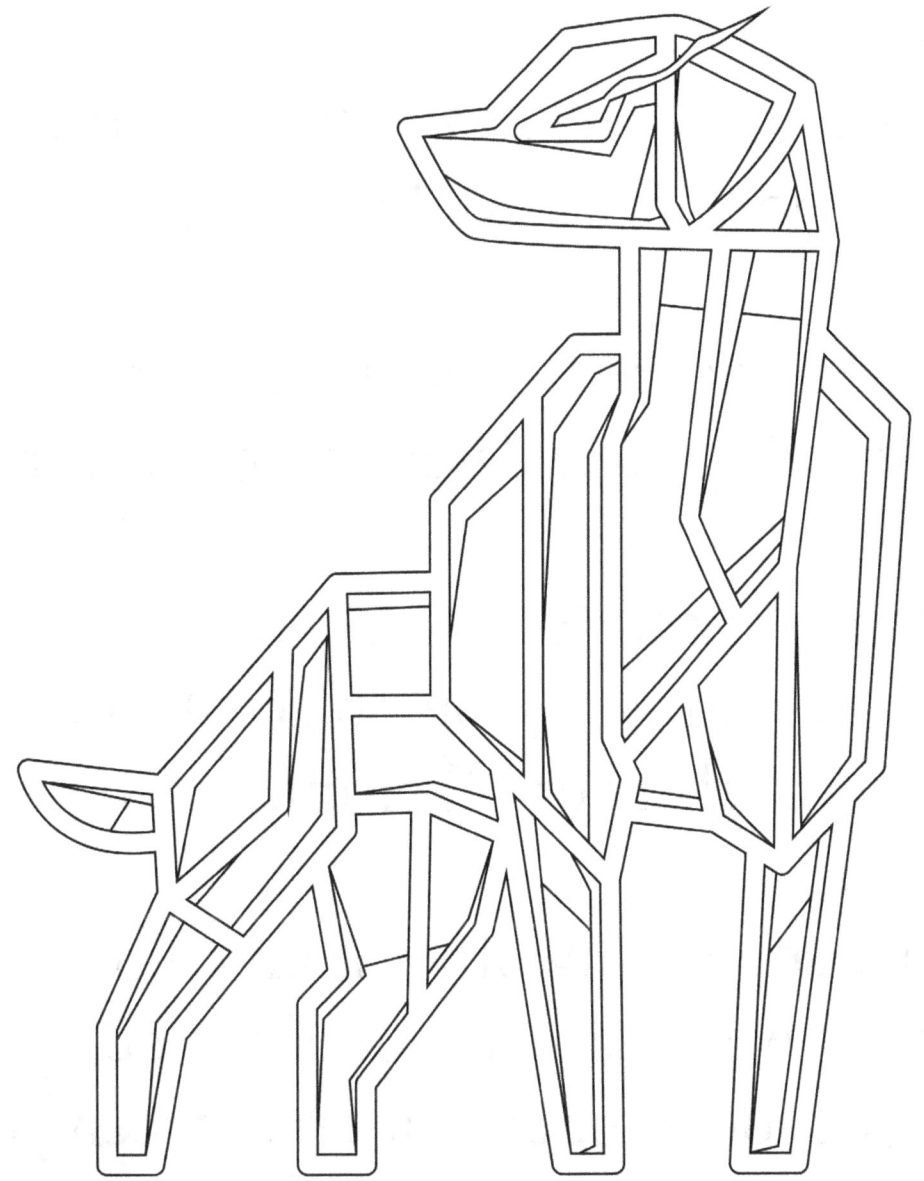

THIS BOOK BELONG TO:

_____

# ABOUT THIS BOOK

*Thank you for purchasing this quality coloring book from Nicholas Nicky!*

Inside this book are 50 unique and fantastic Robot Animal coloring pages designed especially for adult.

Each image is on its own page with a BLANK backside to help avoid color bleed-through if you color with markers or other ink based pens.

If you use something other than colored pencils or crayons, we also recom-mend placing a sheet of paper or some other blotter between your coloring page and the one beneath it while you work.

We hope you enjoy your
Robot Animal Coloring Book!

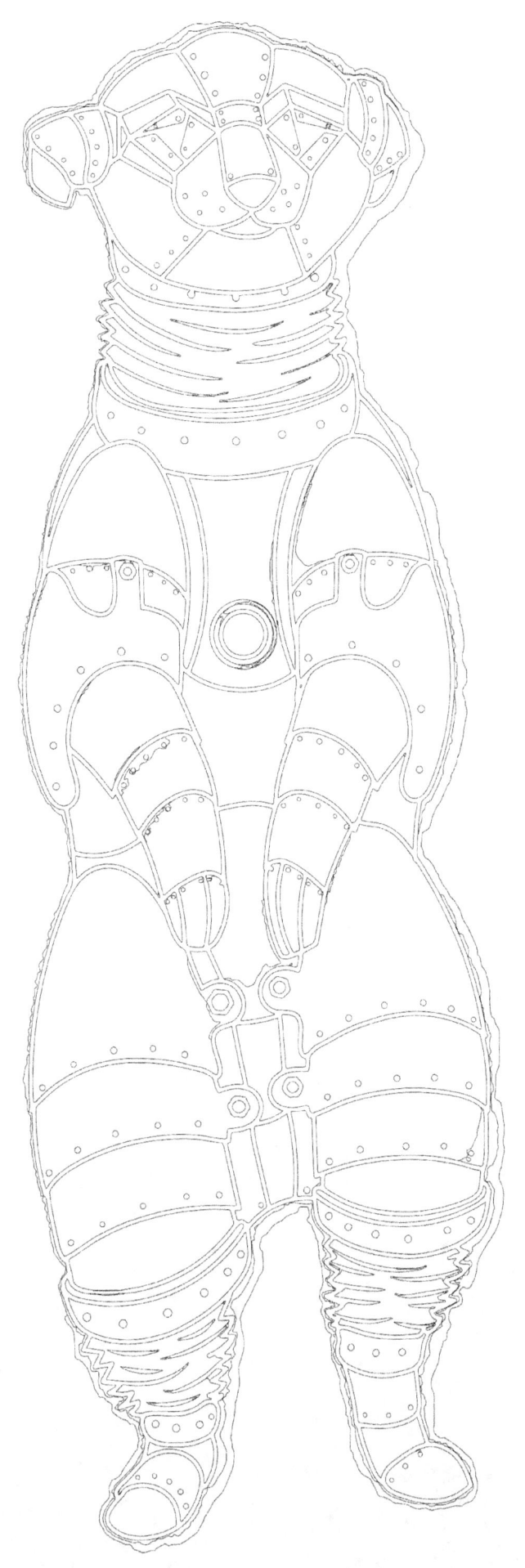

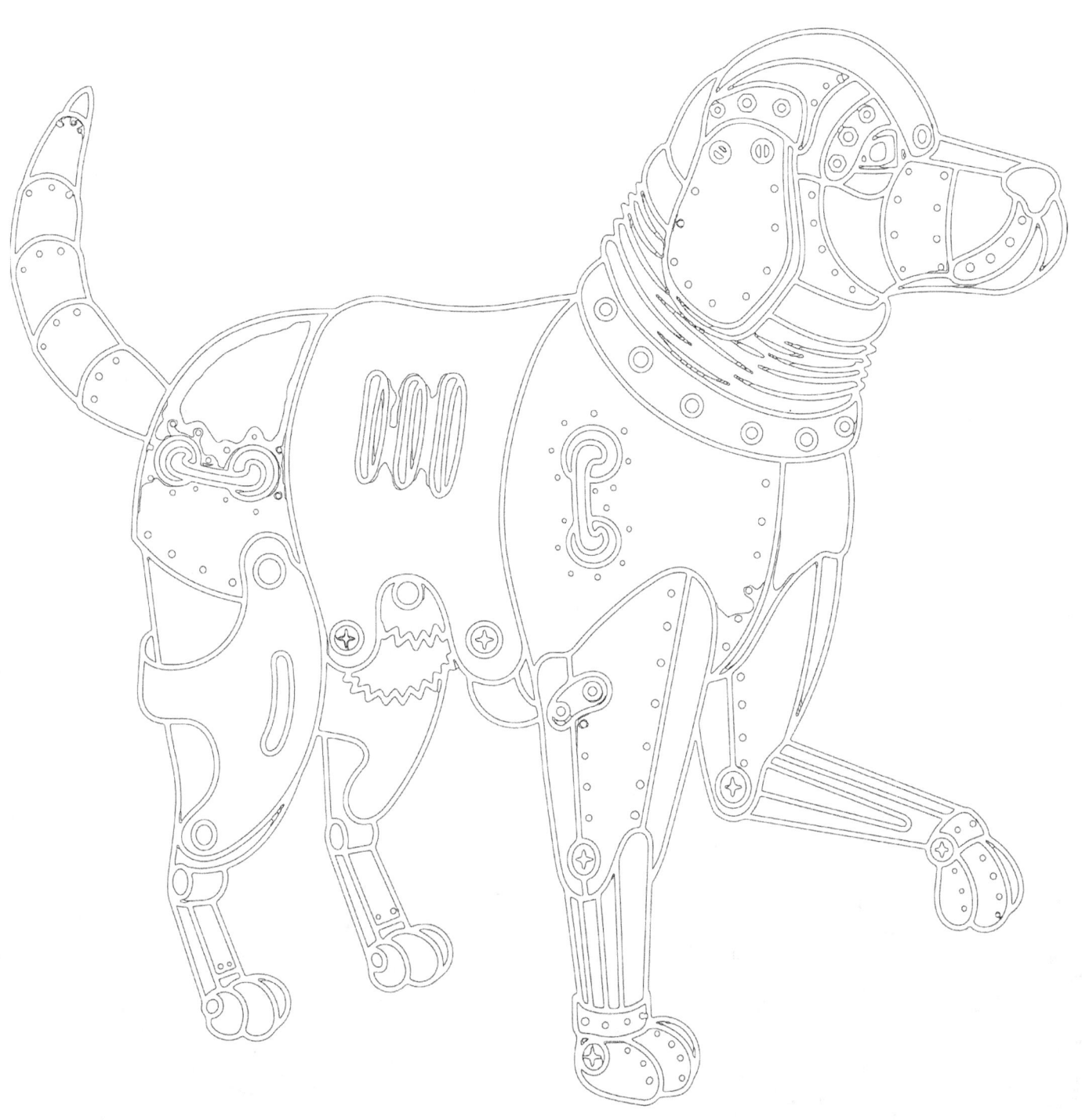

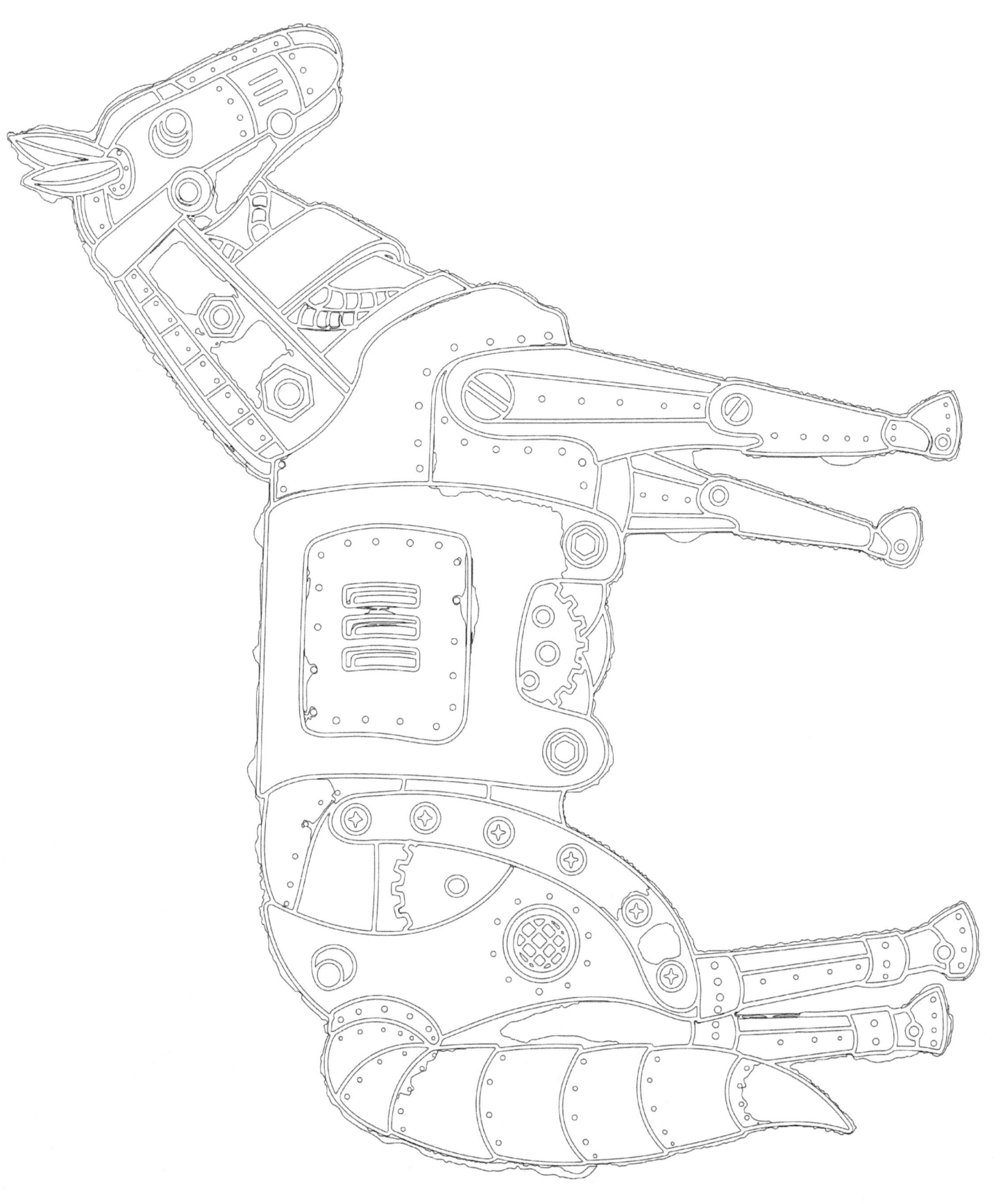

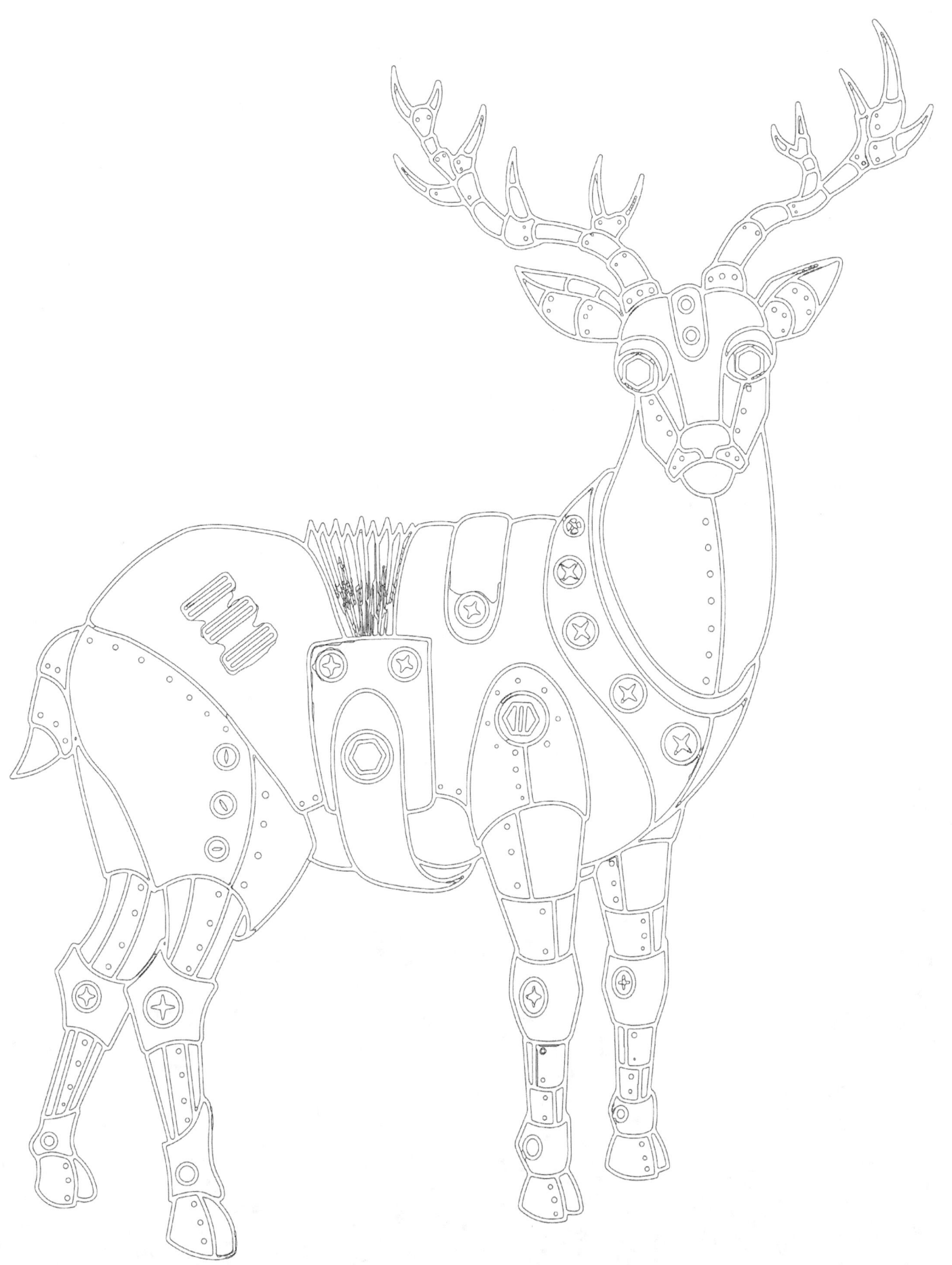

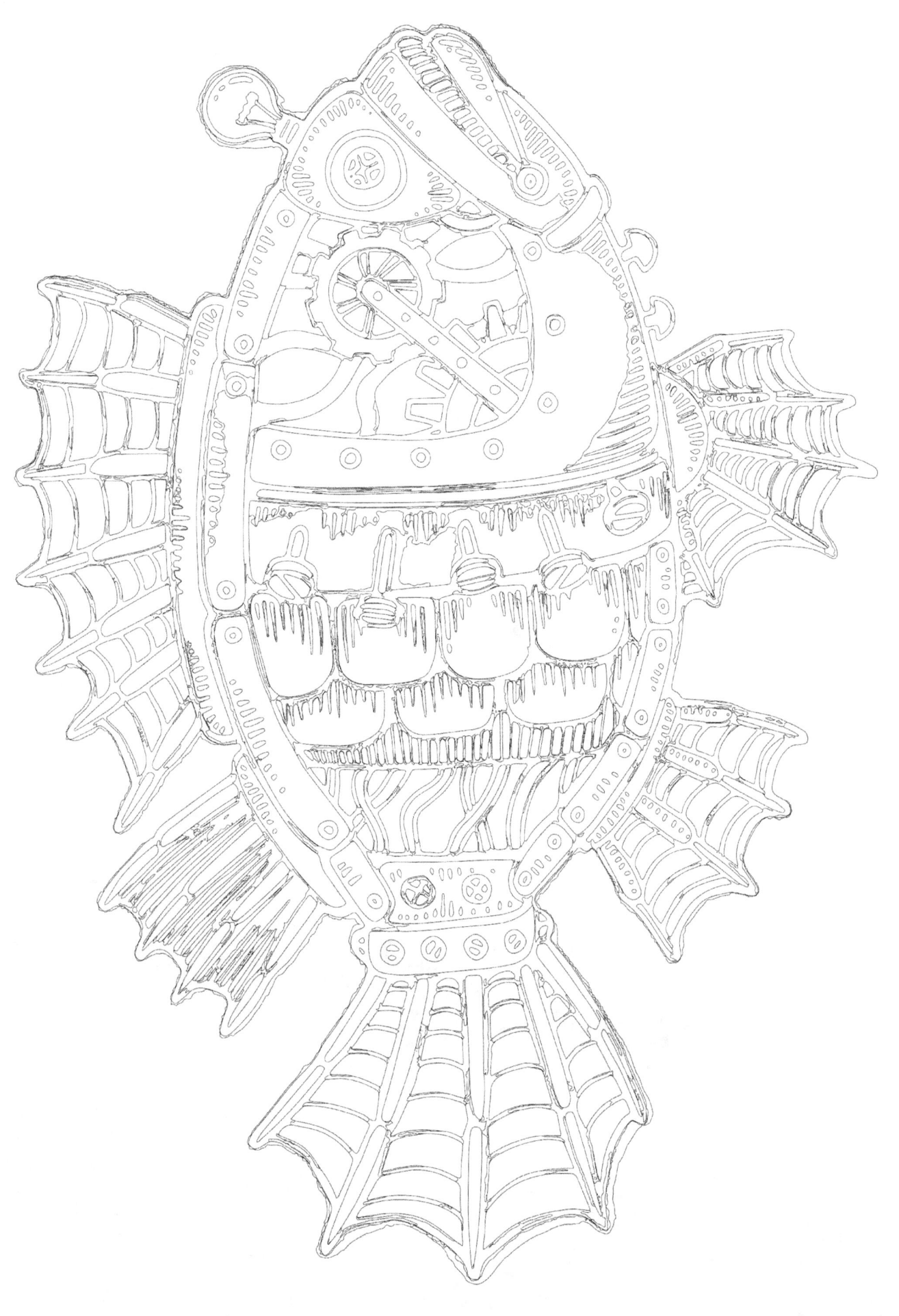

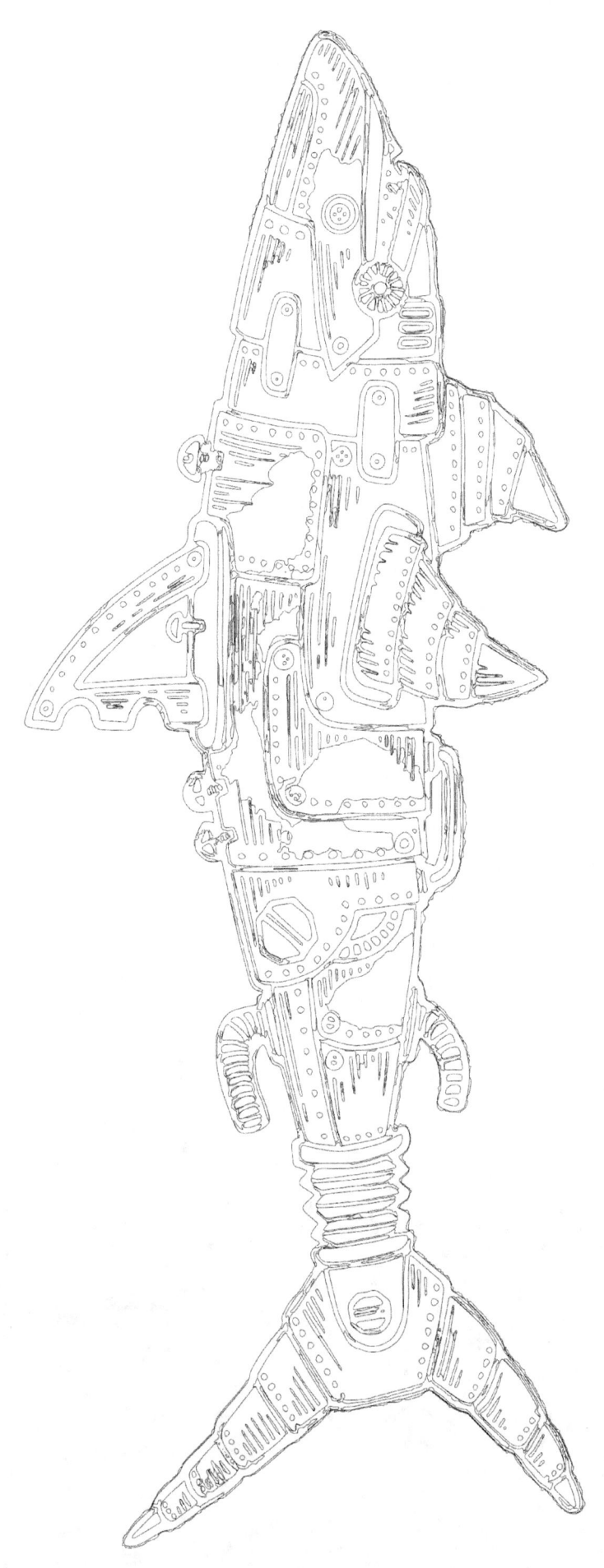

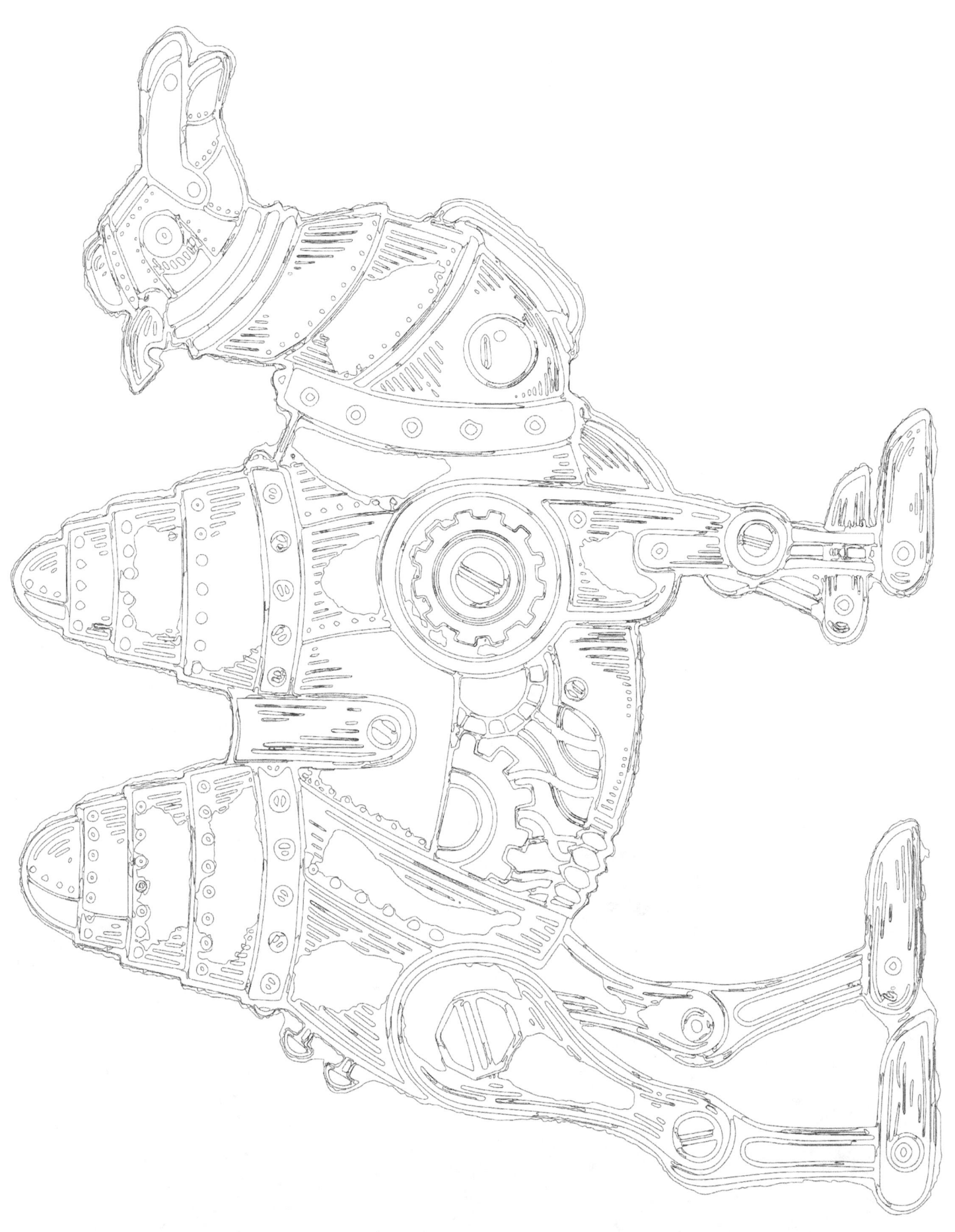

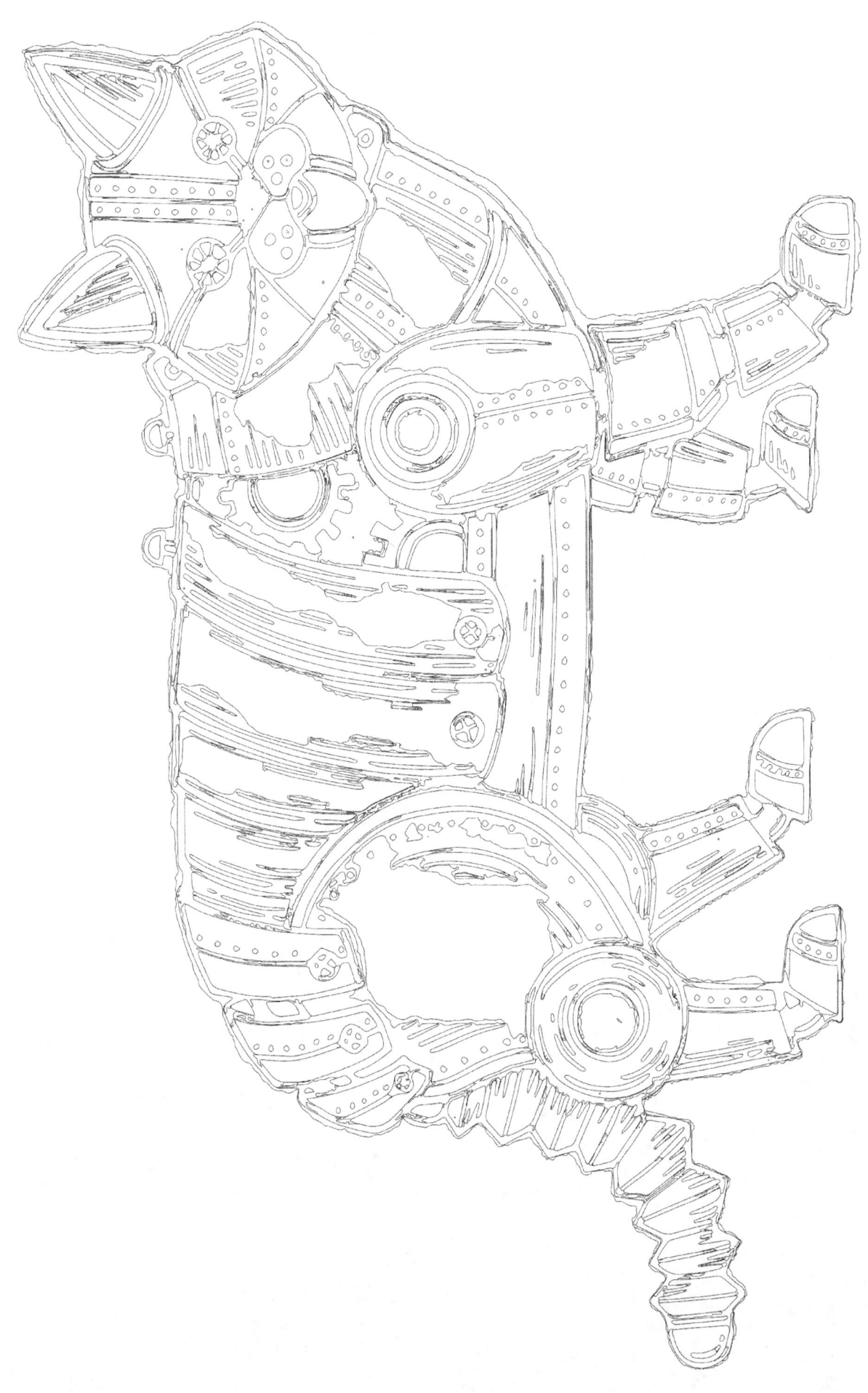

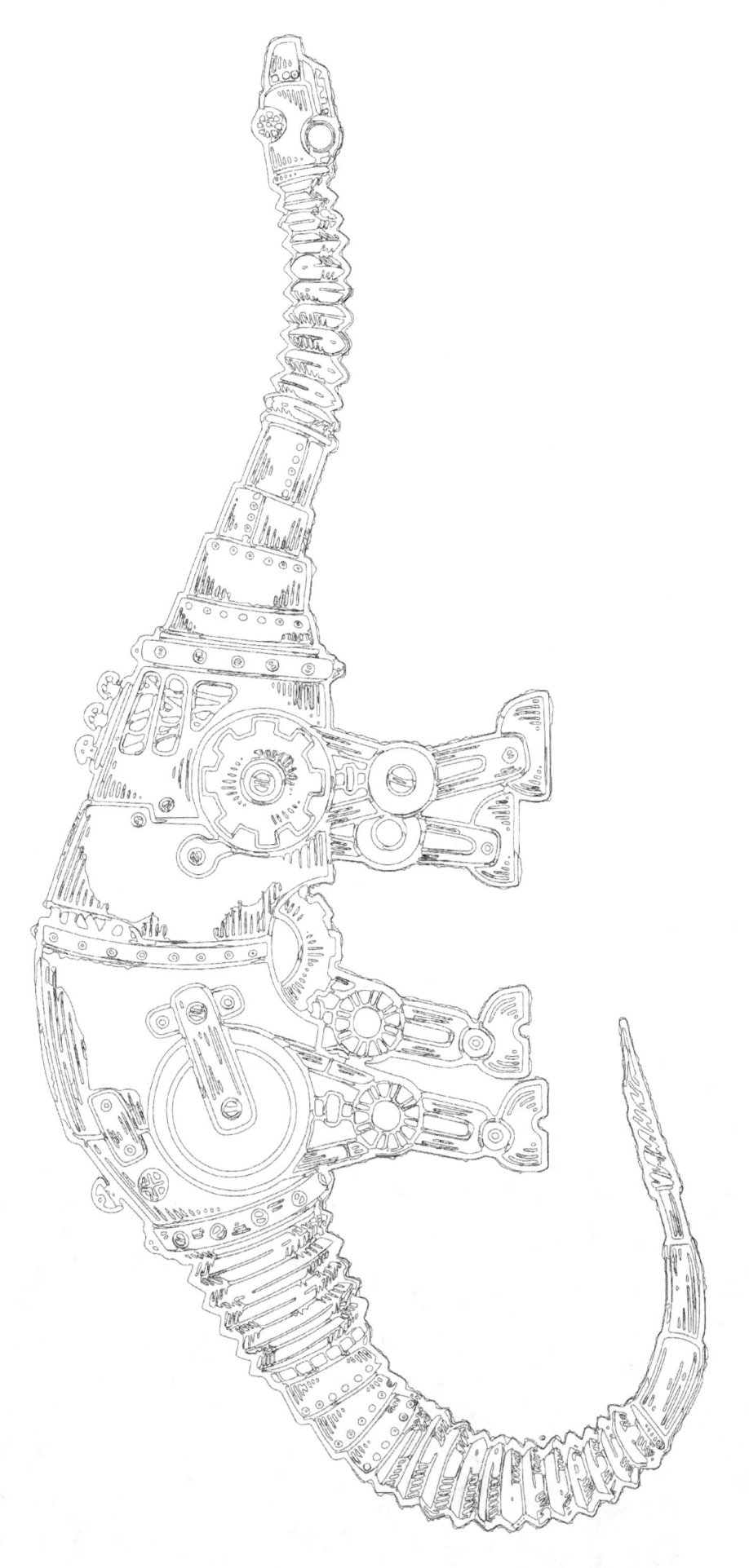

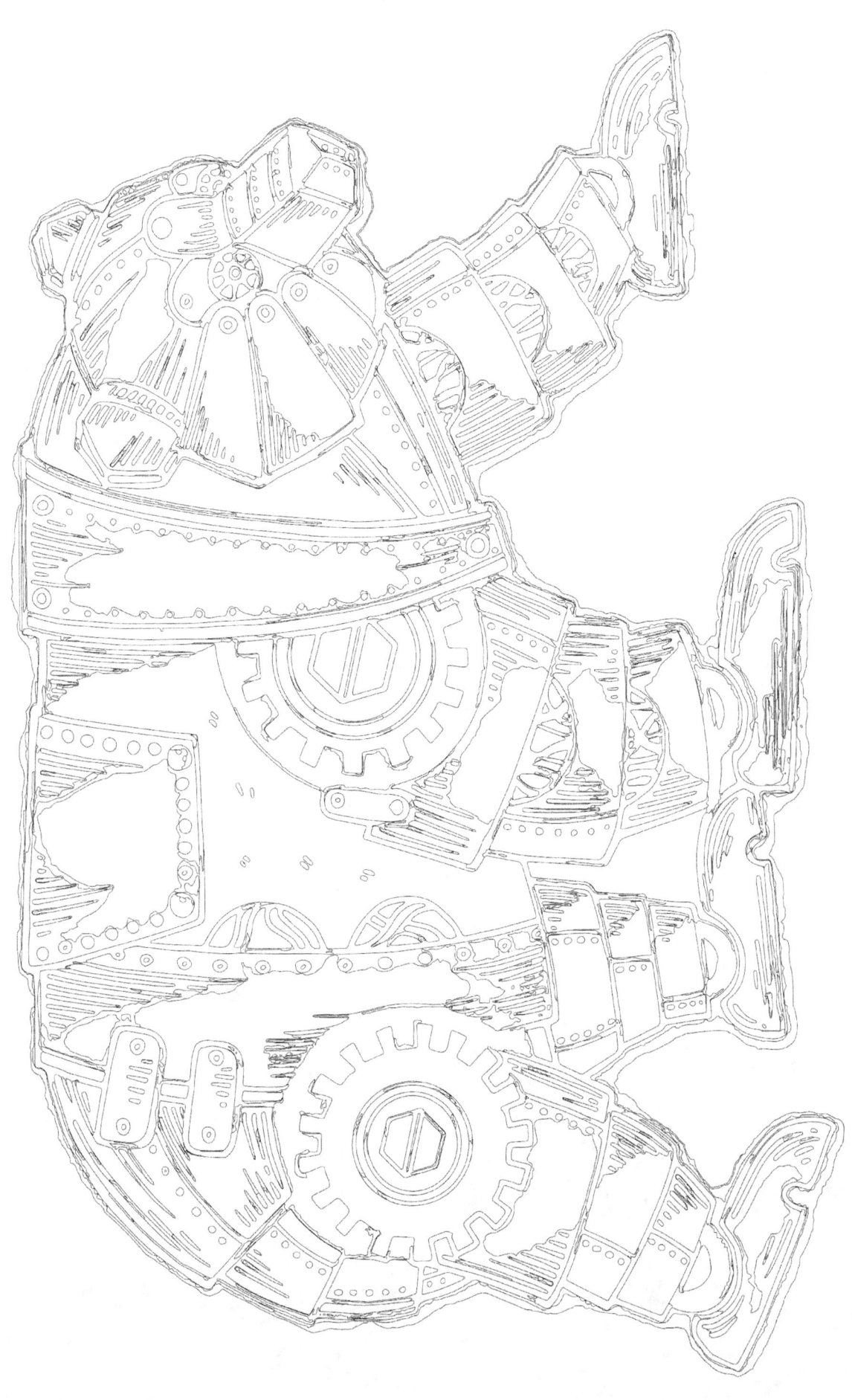

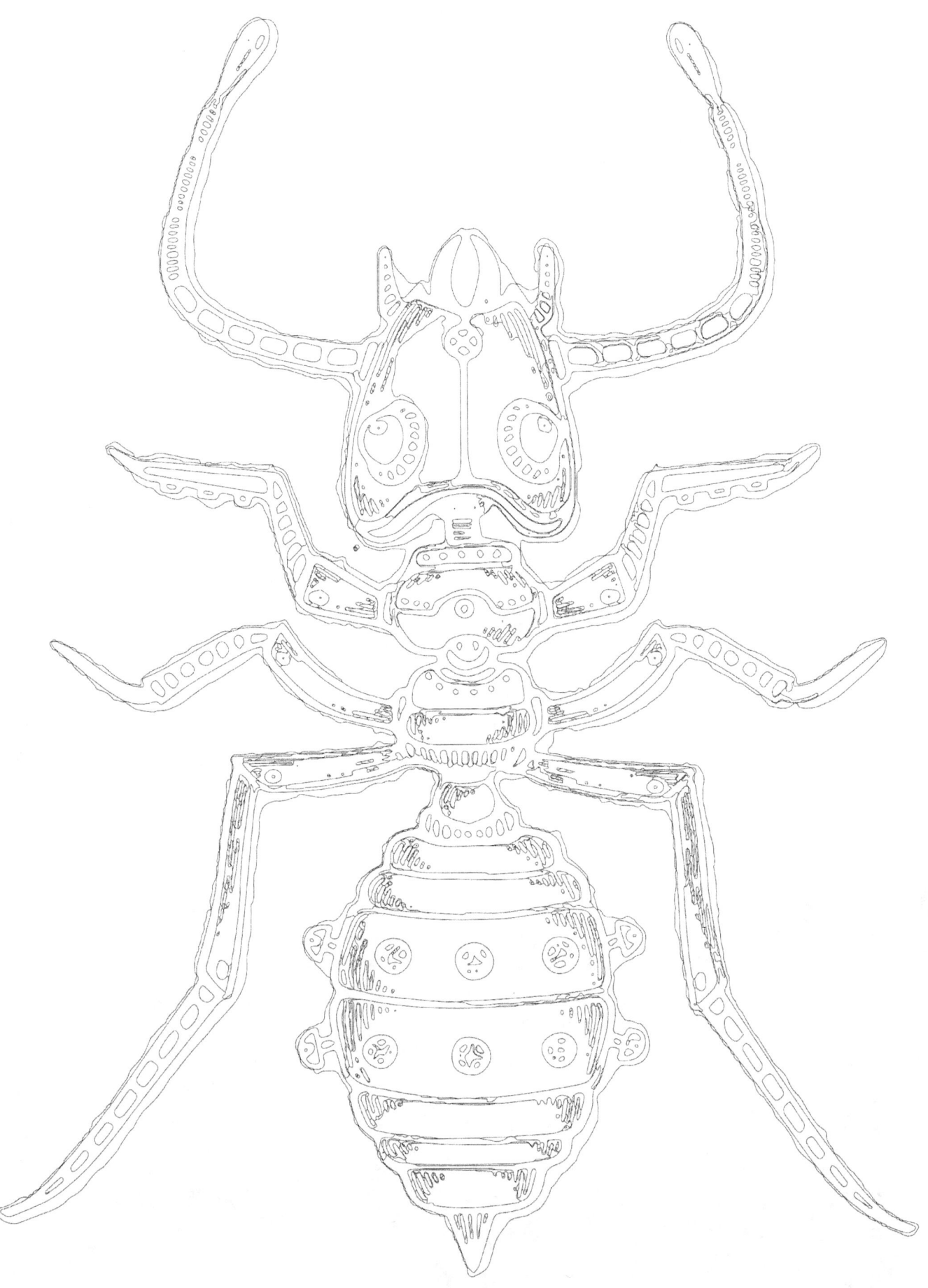

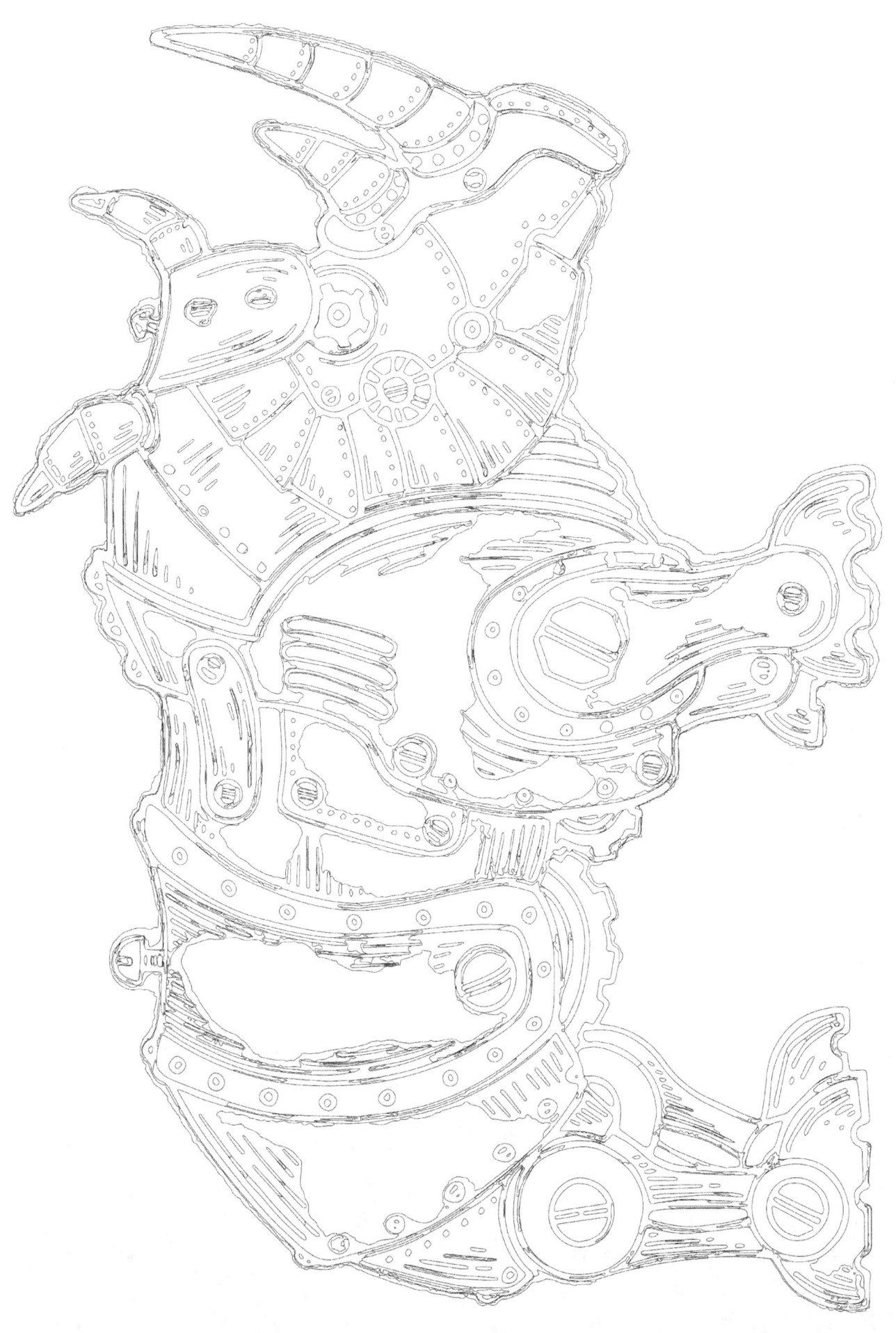

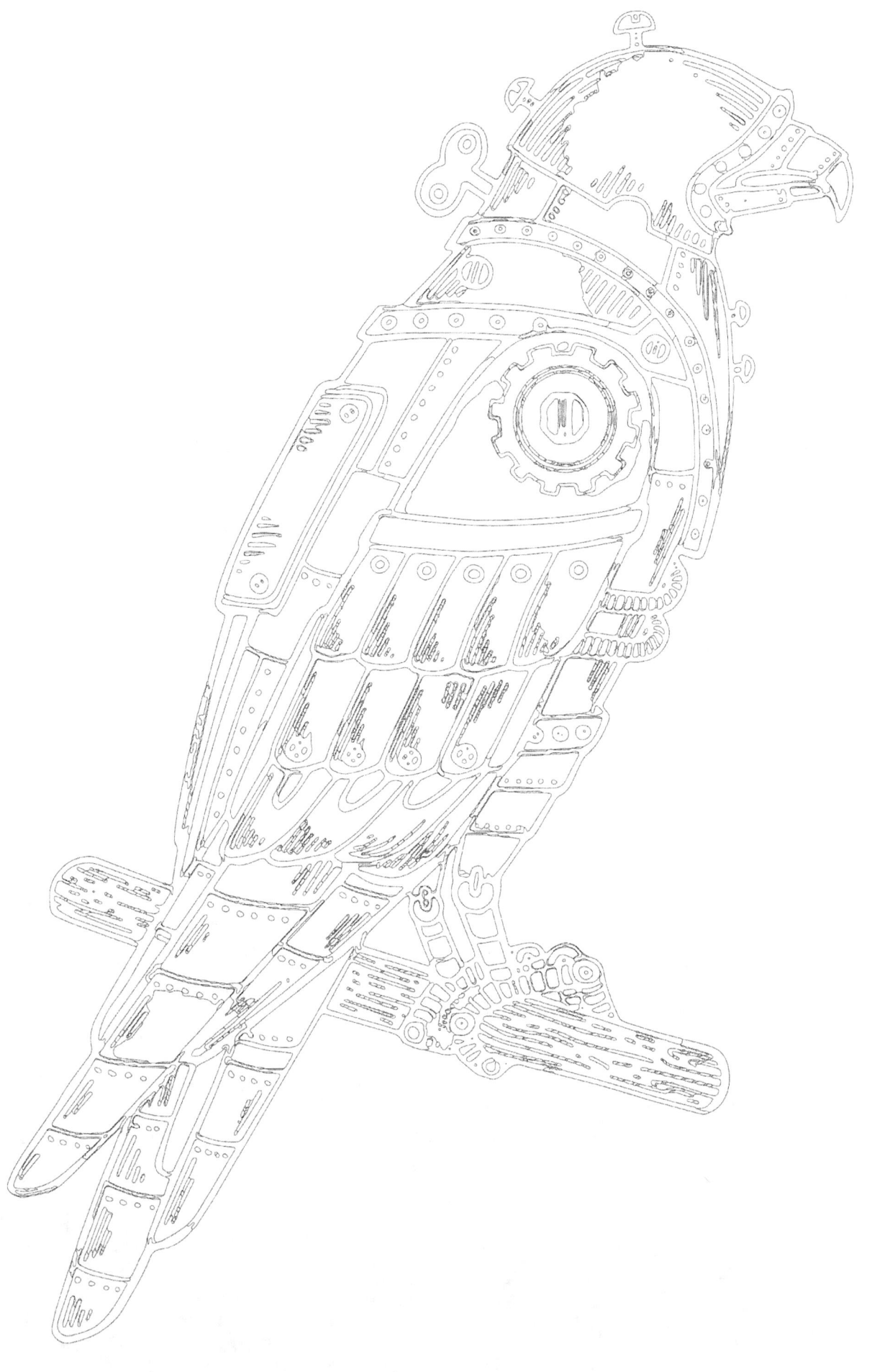

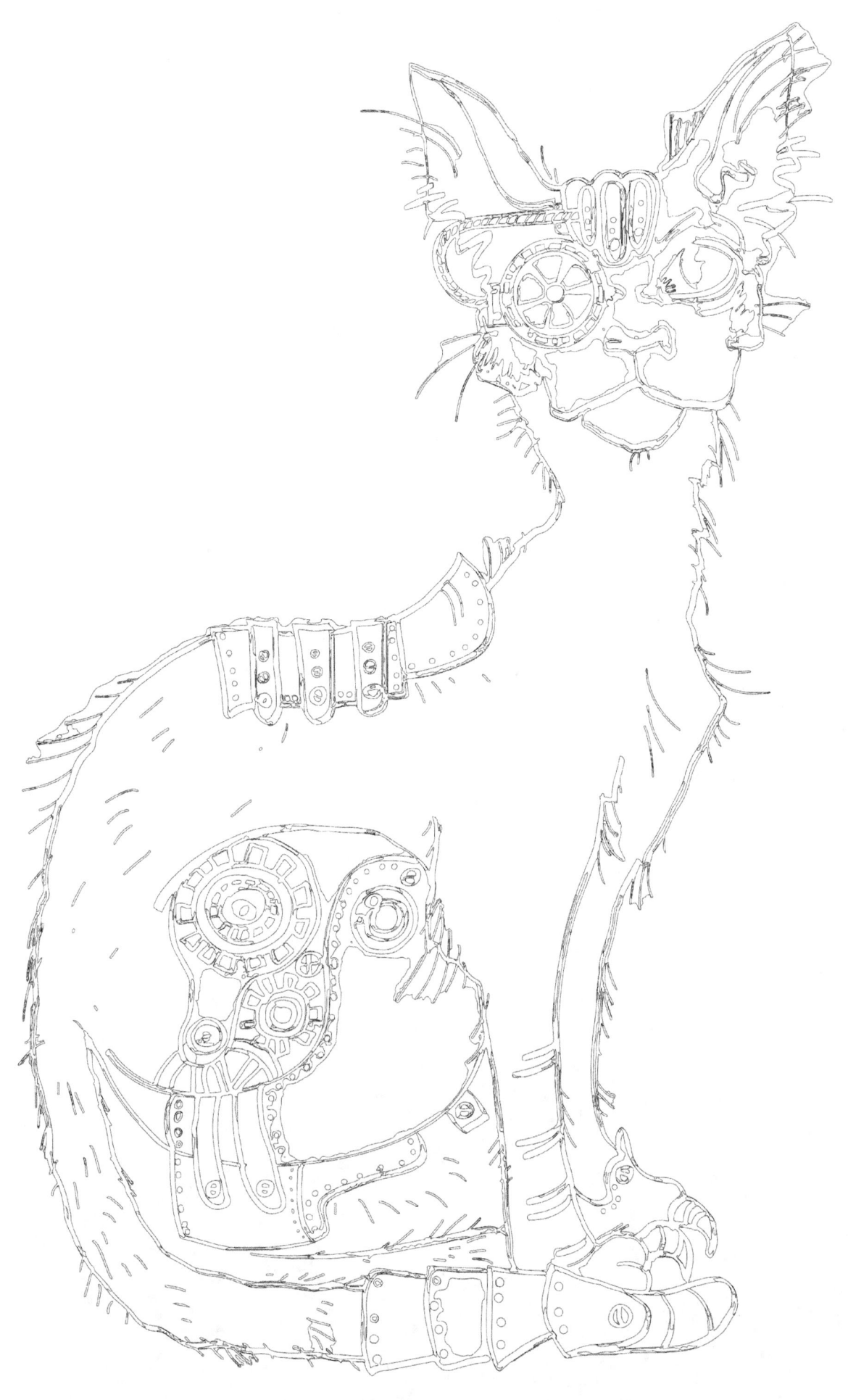

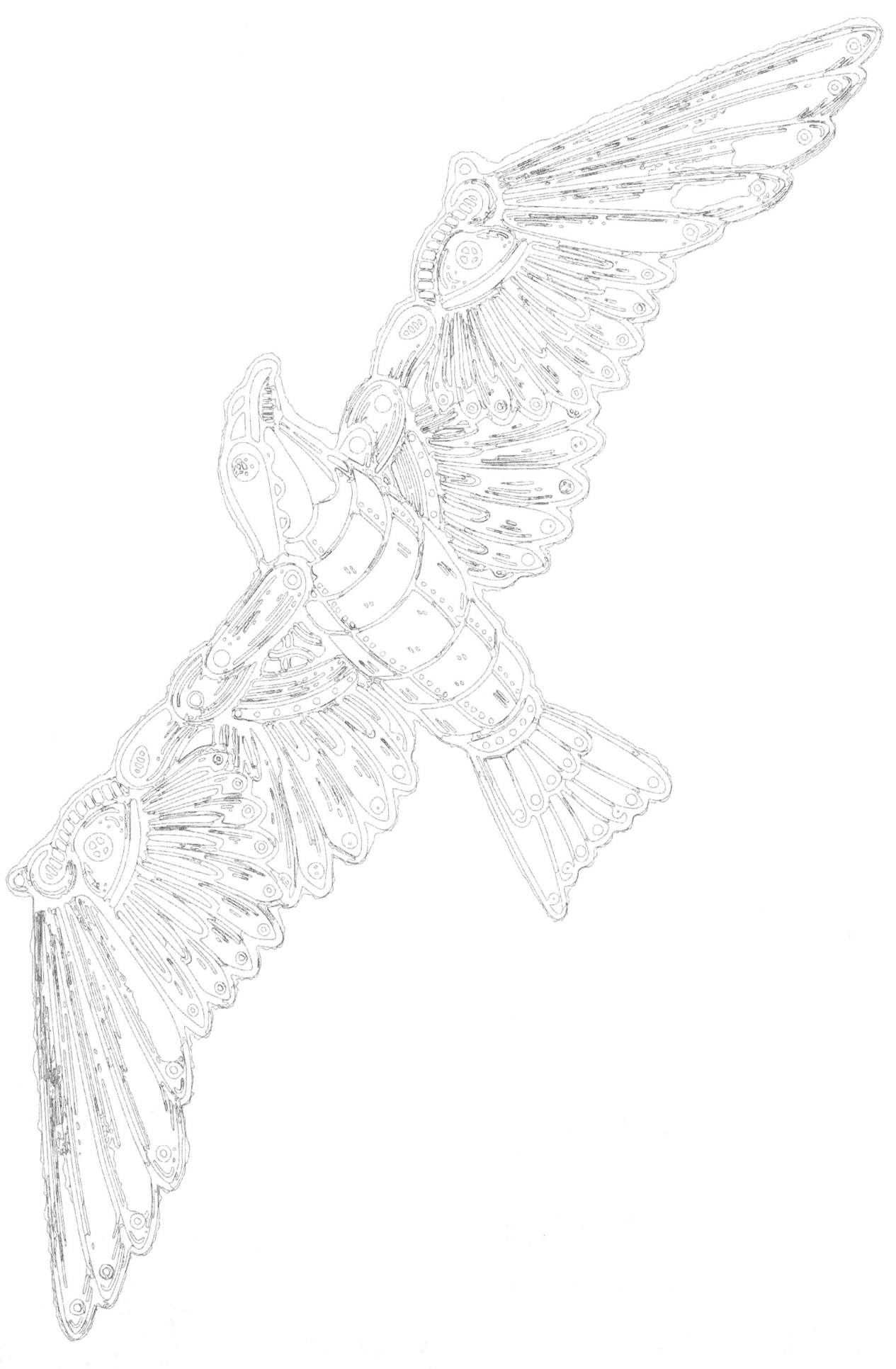

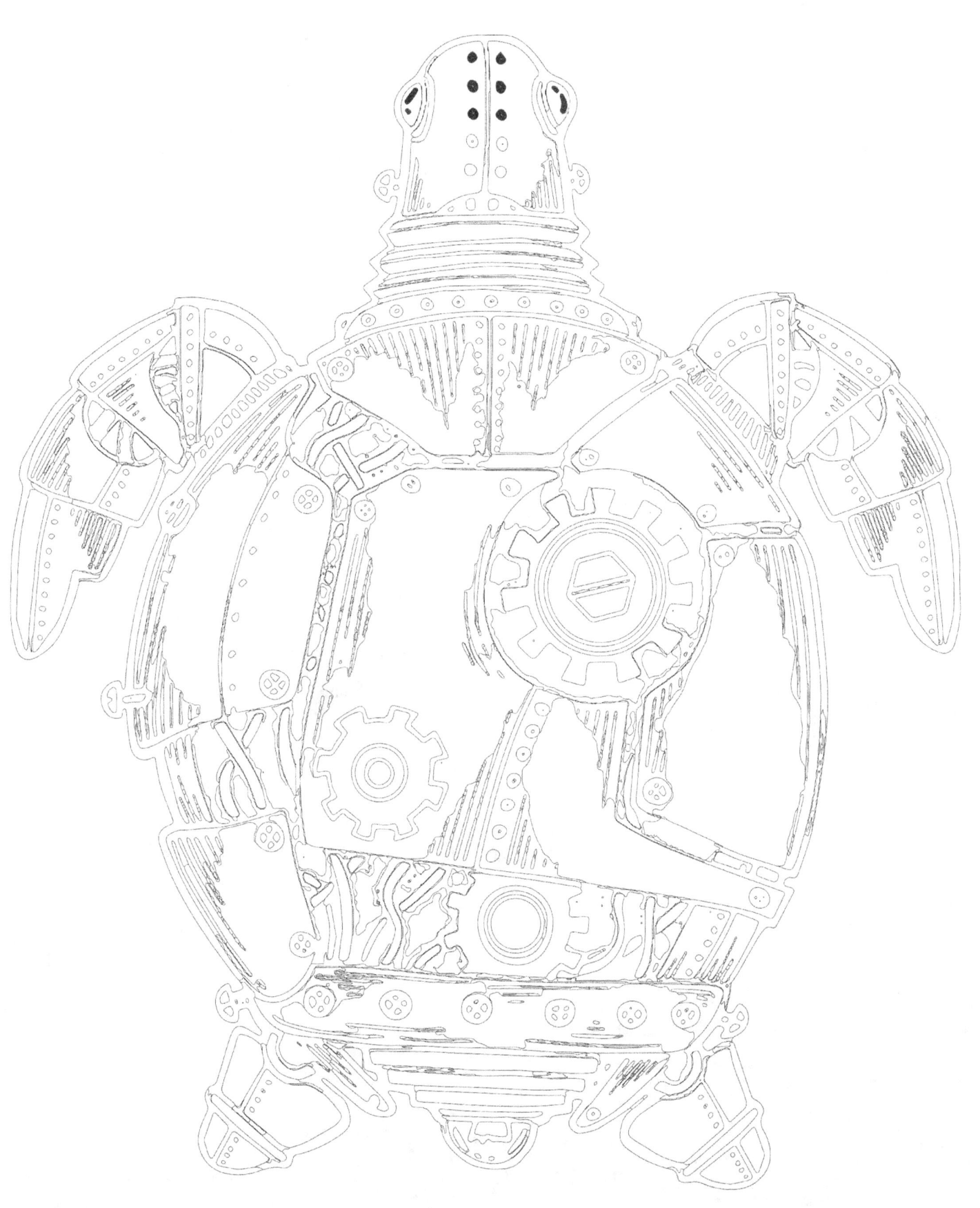

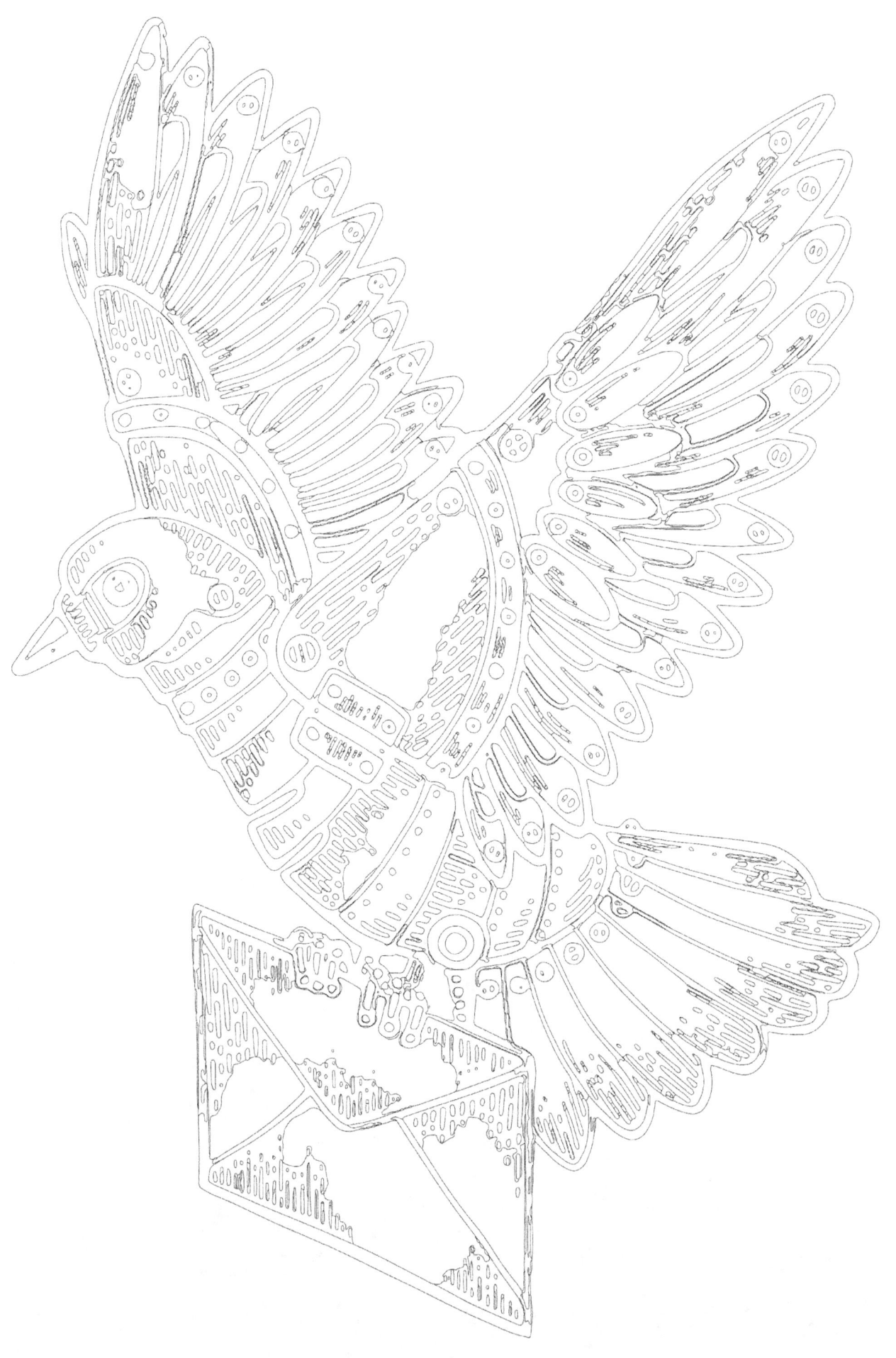

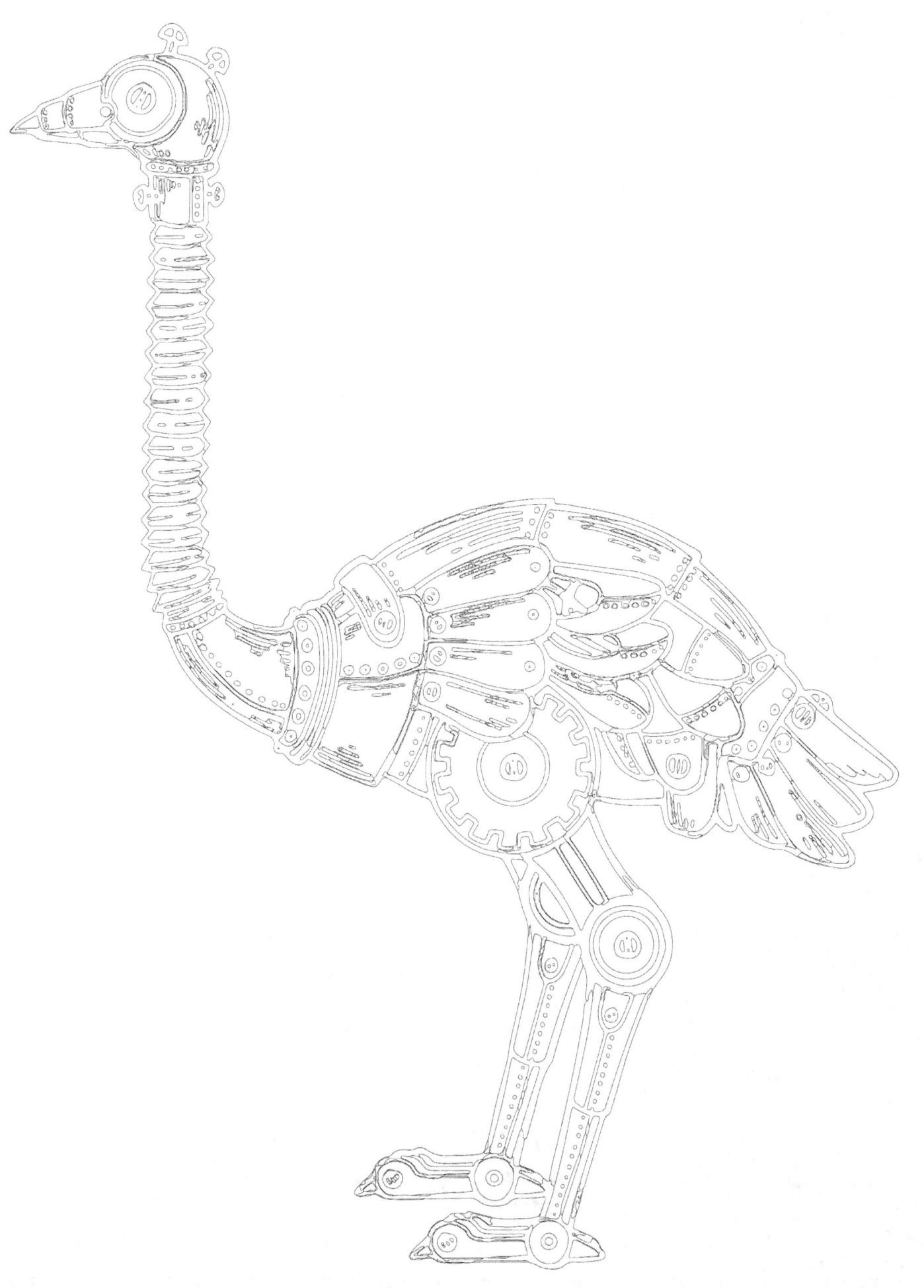

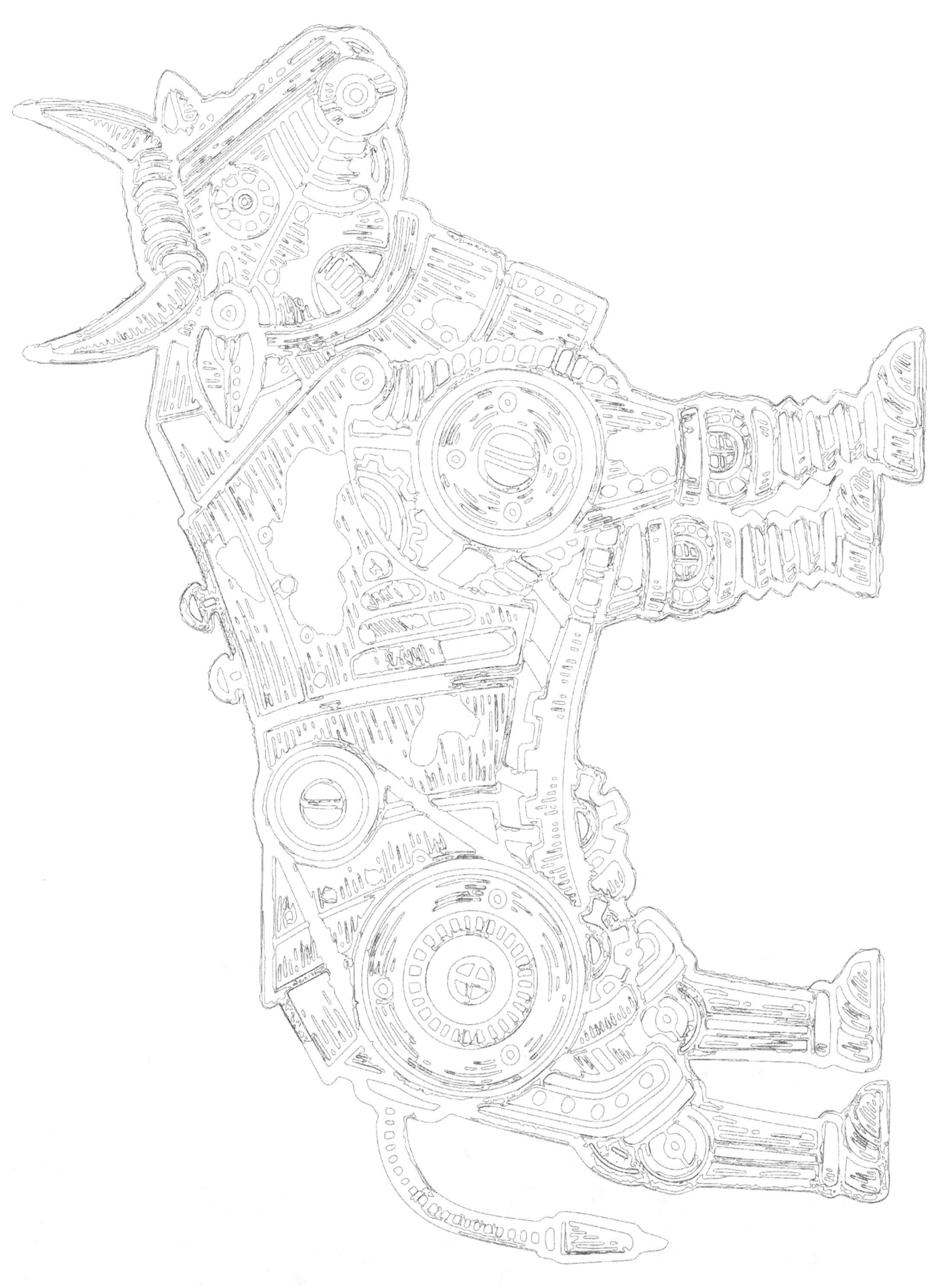

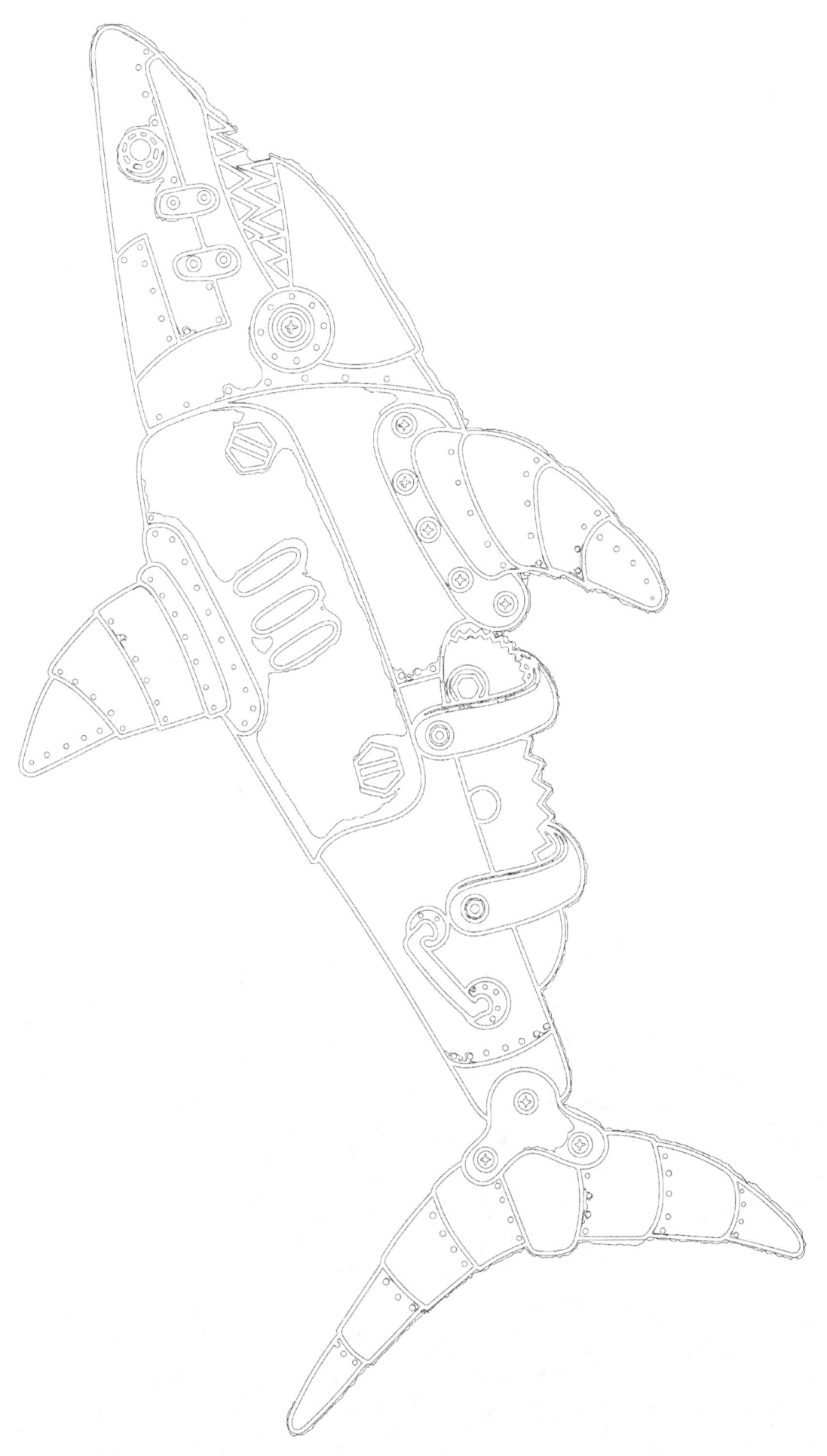

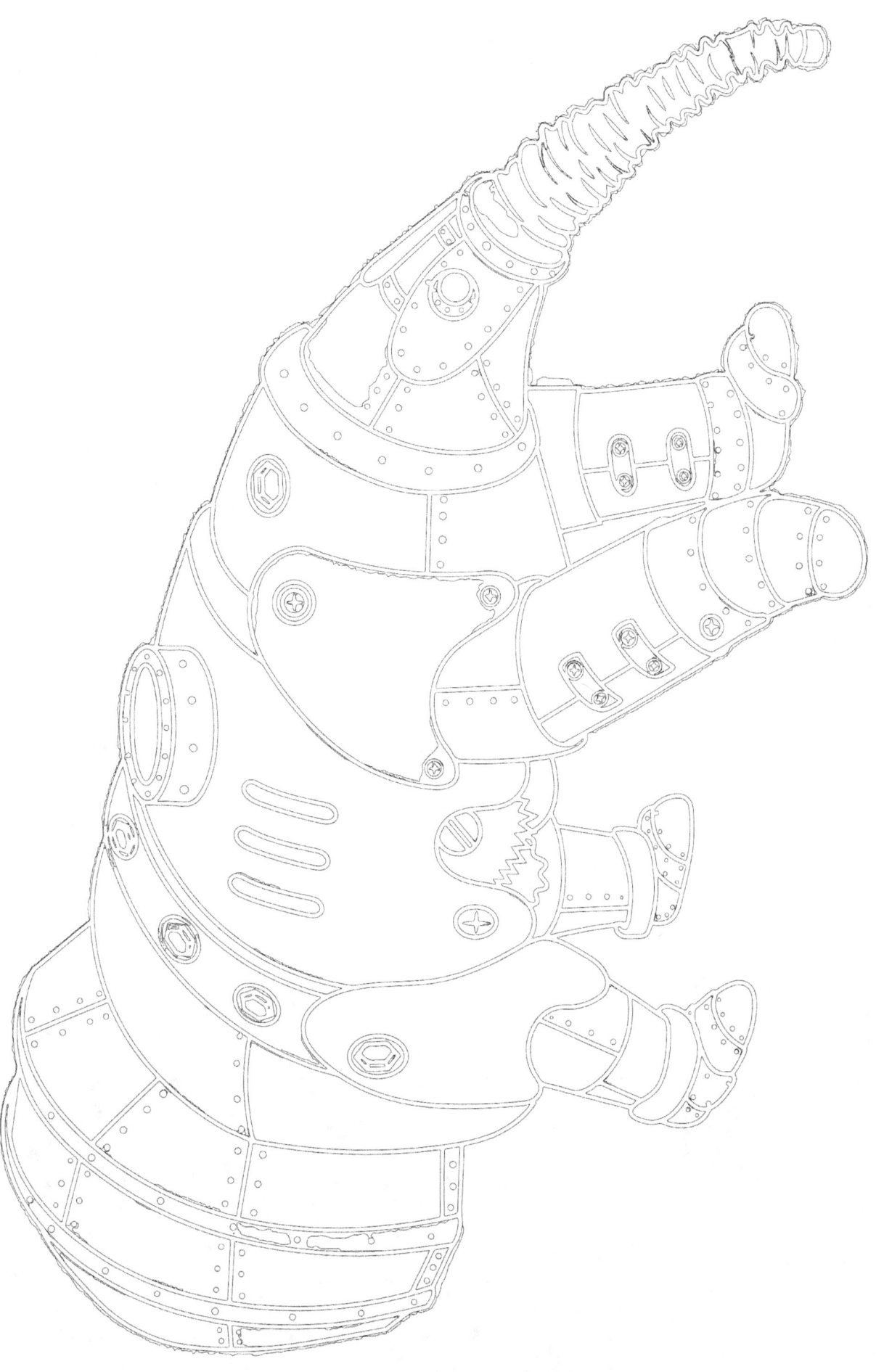

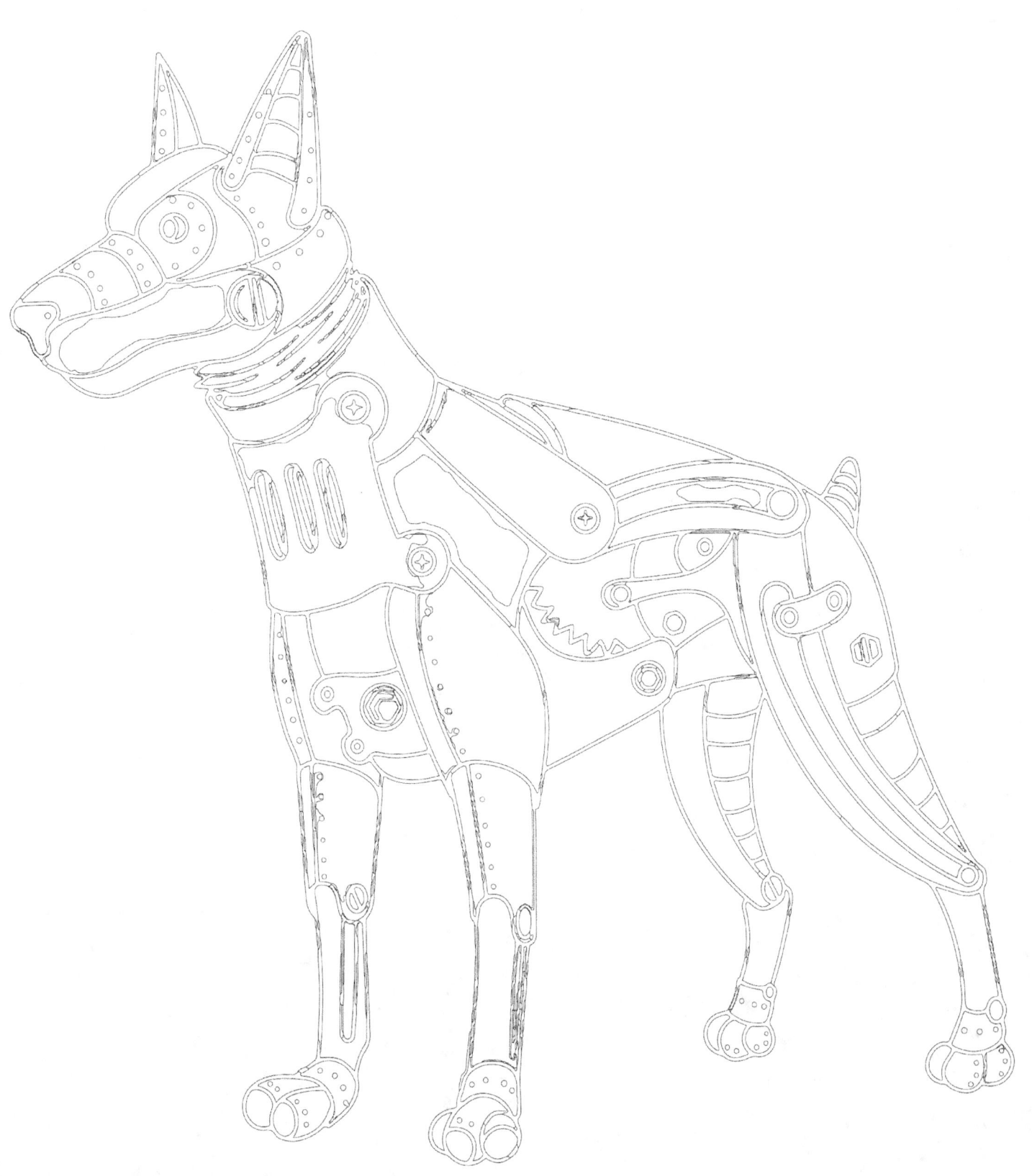

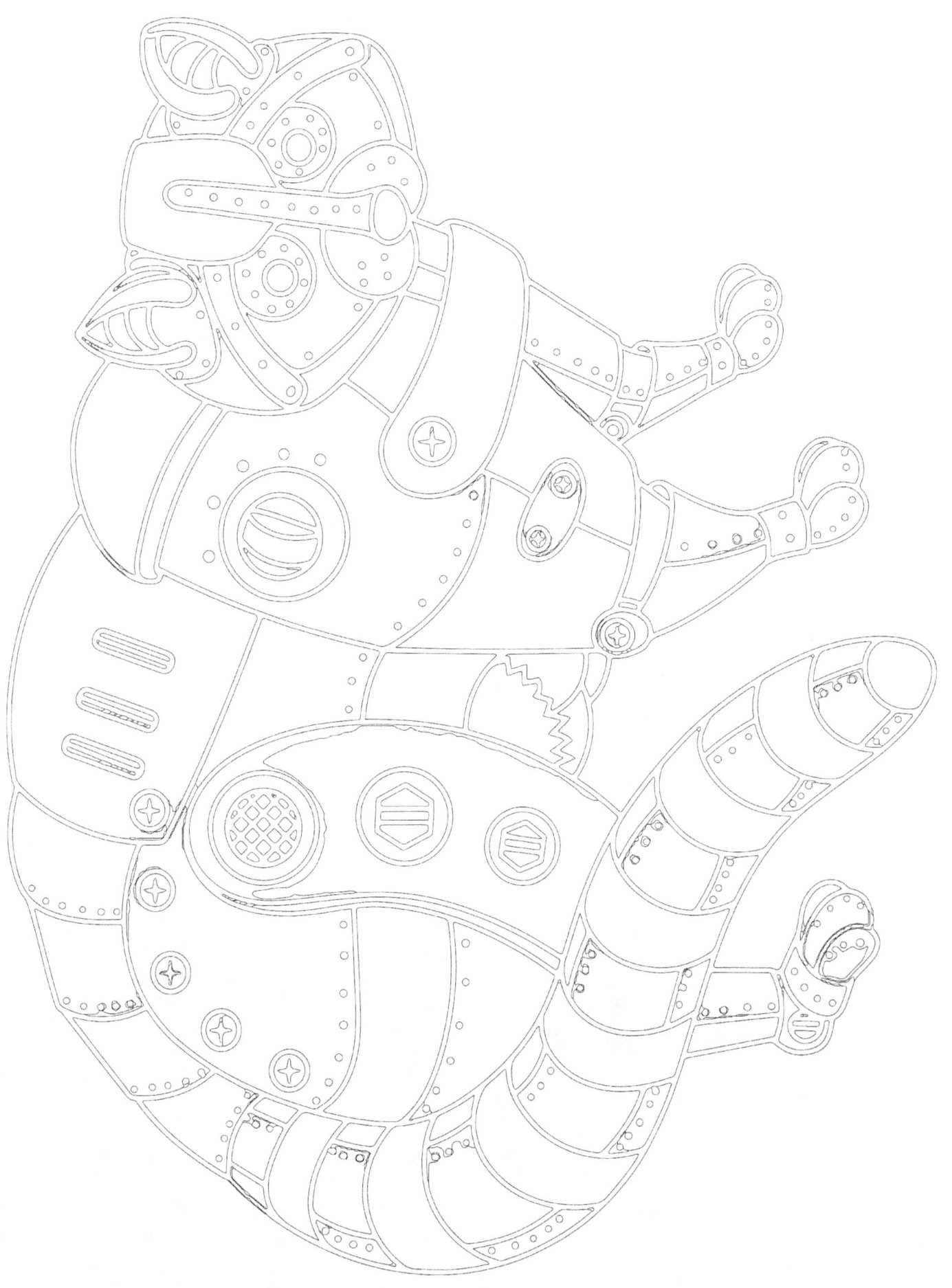

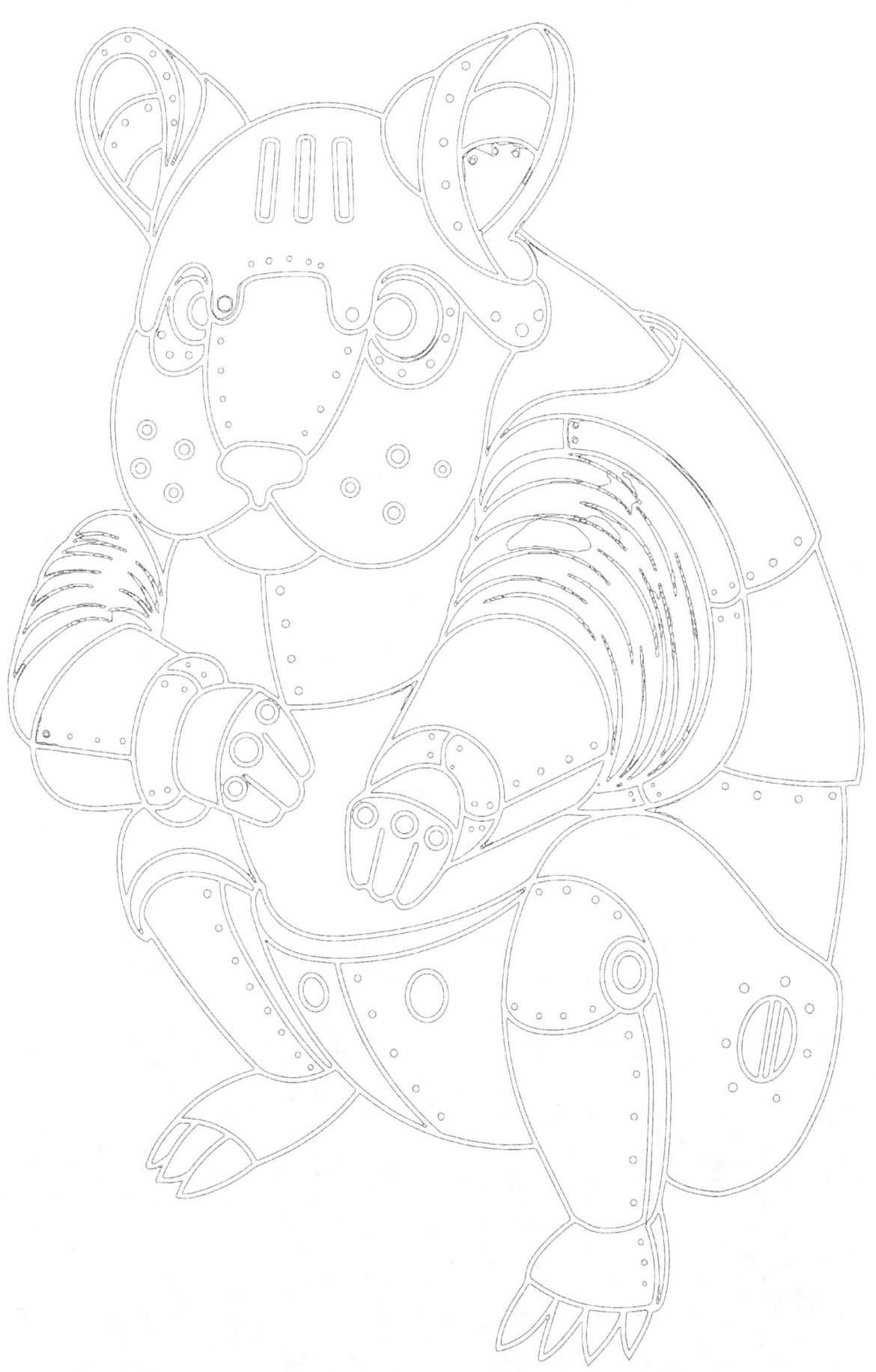

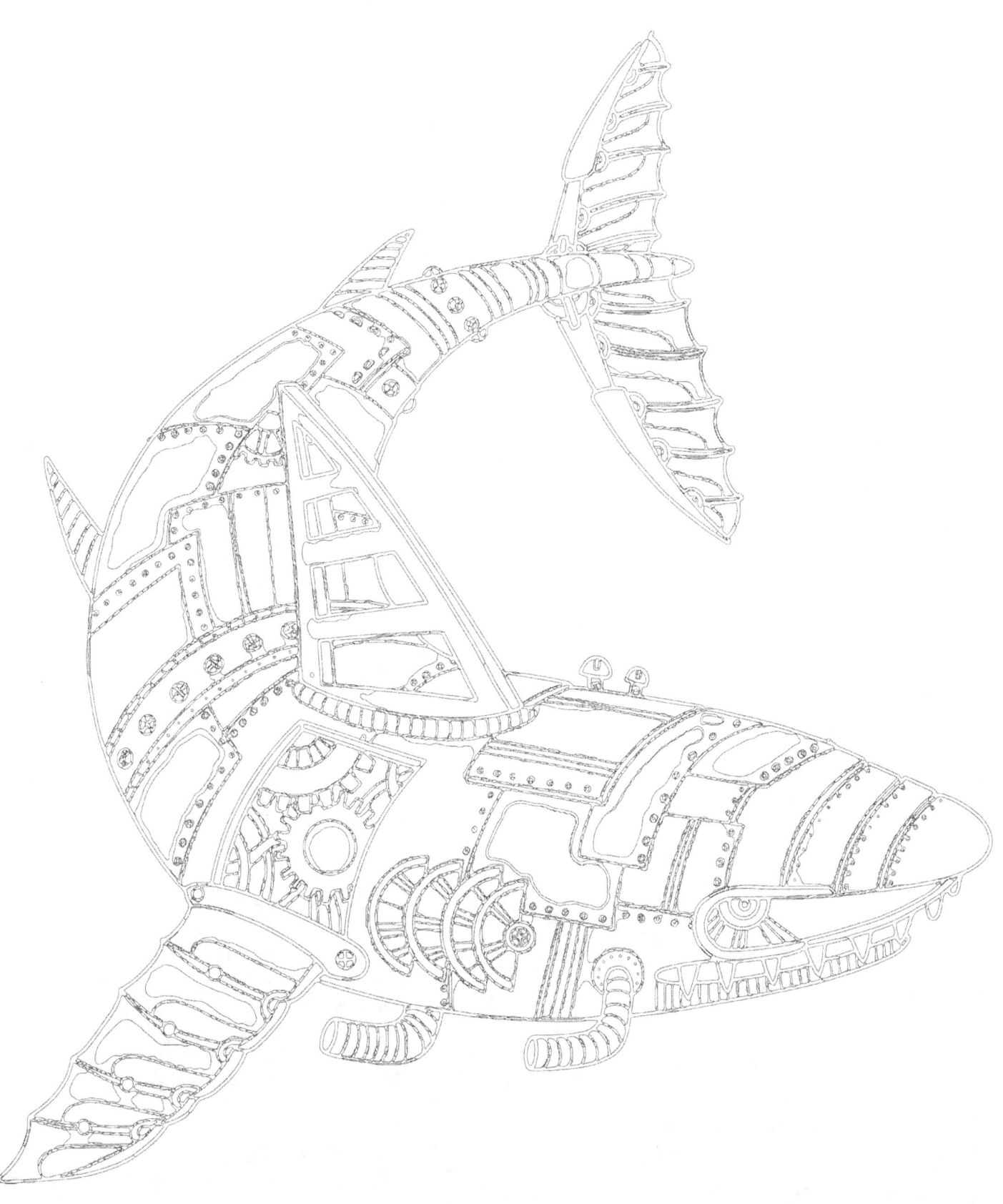

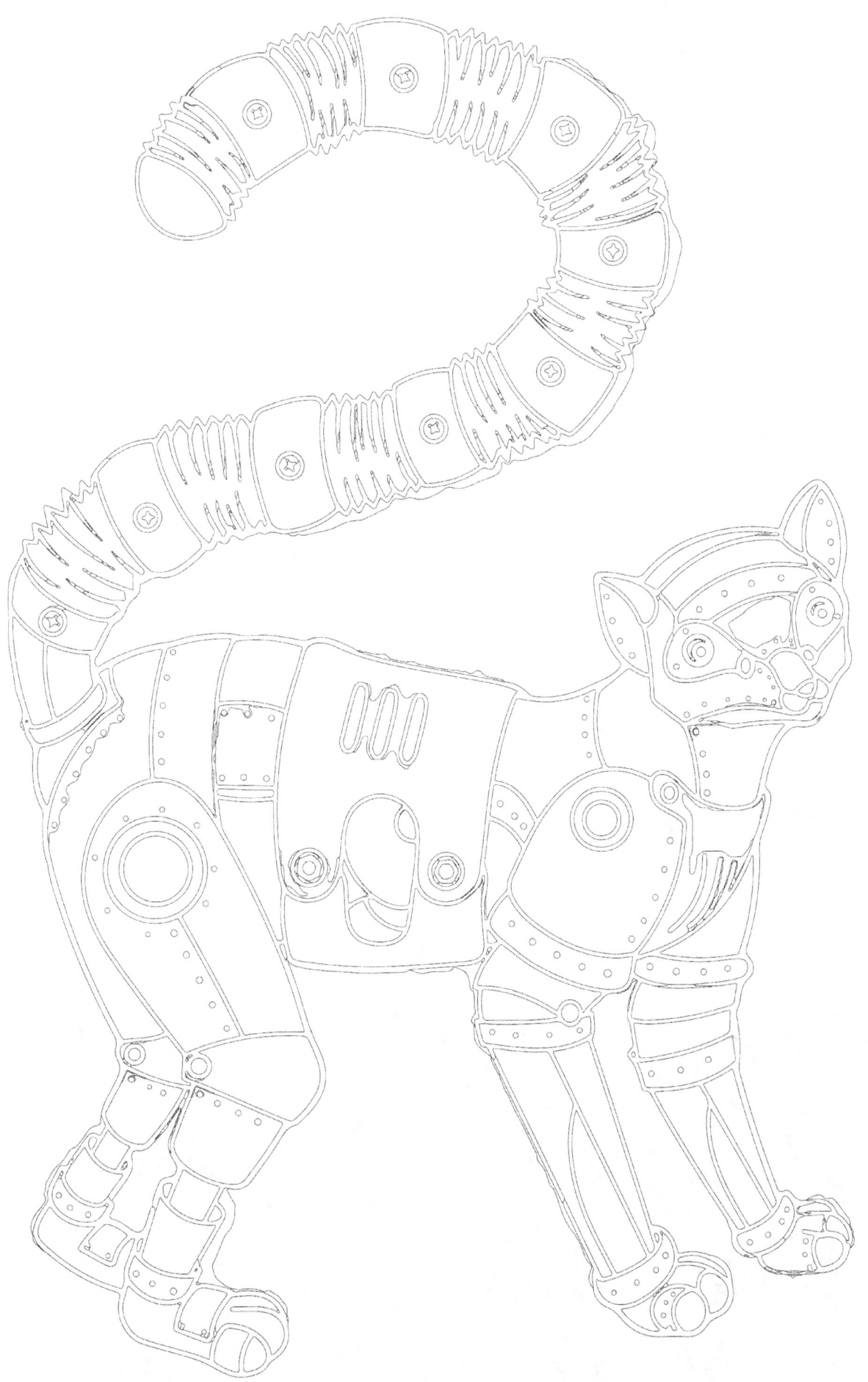

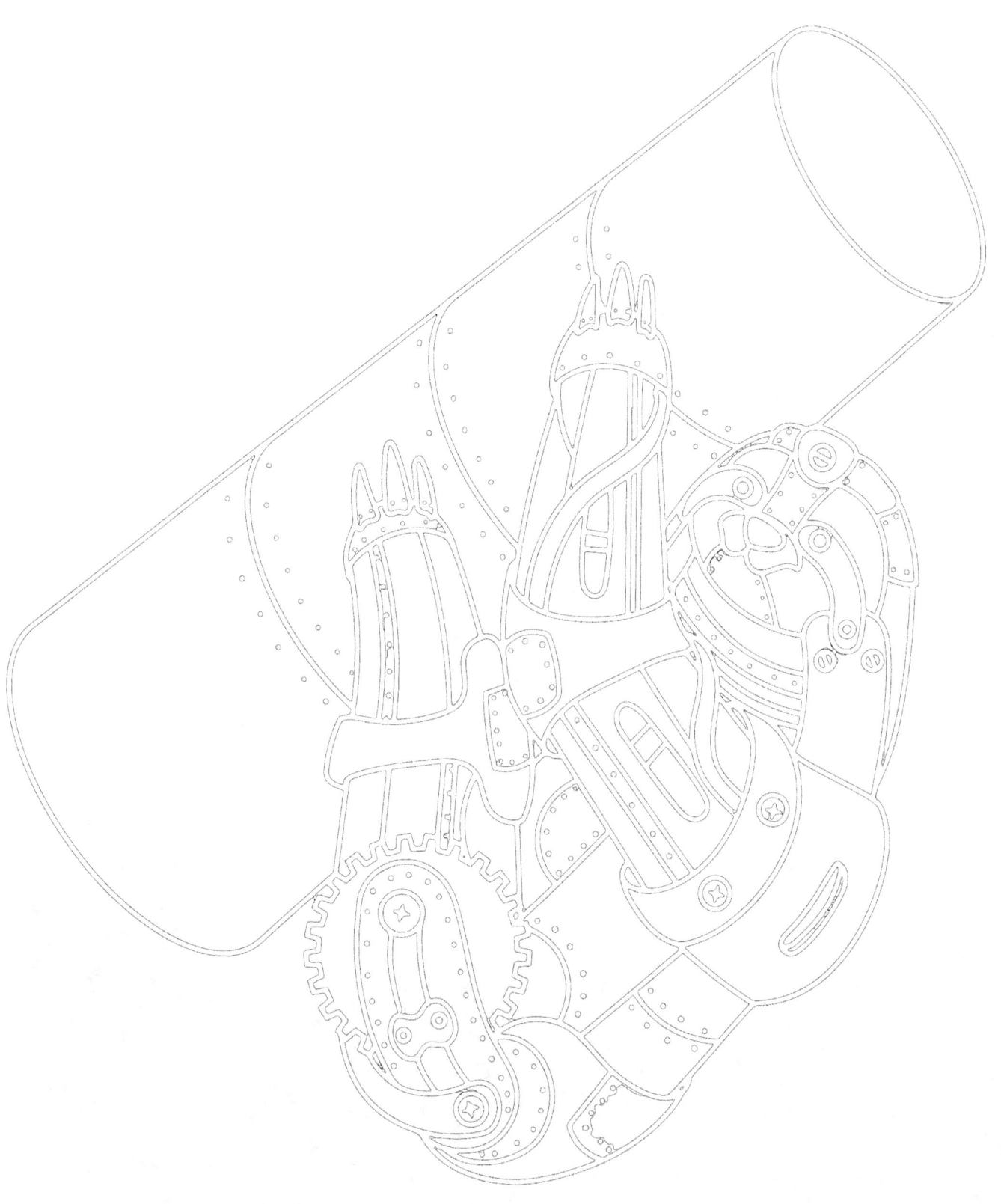

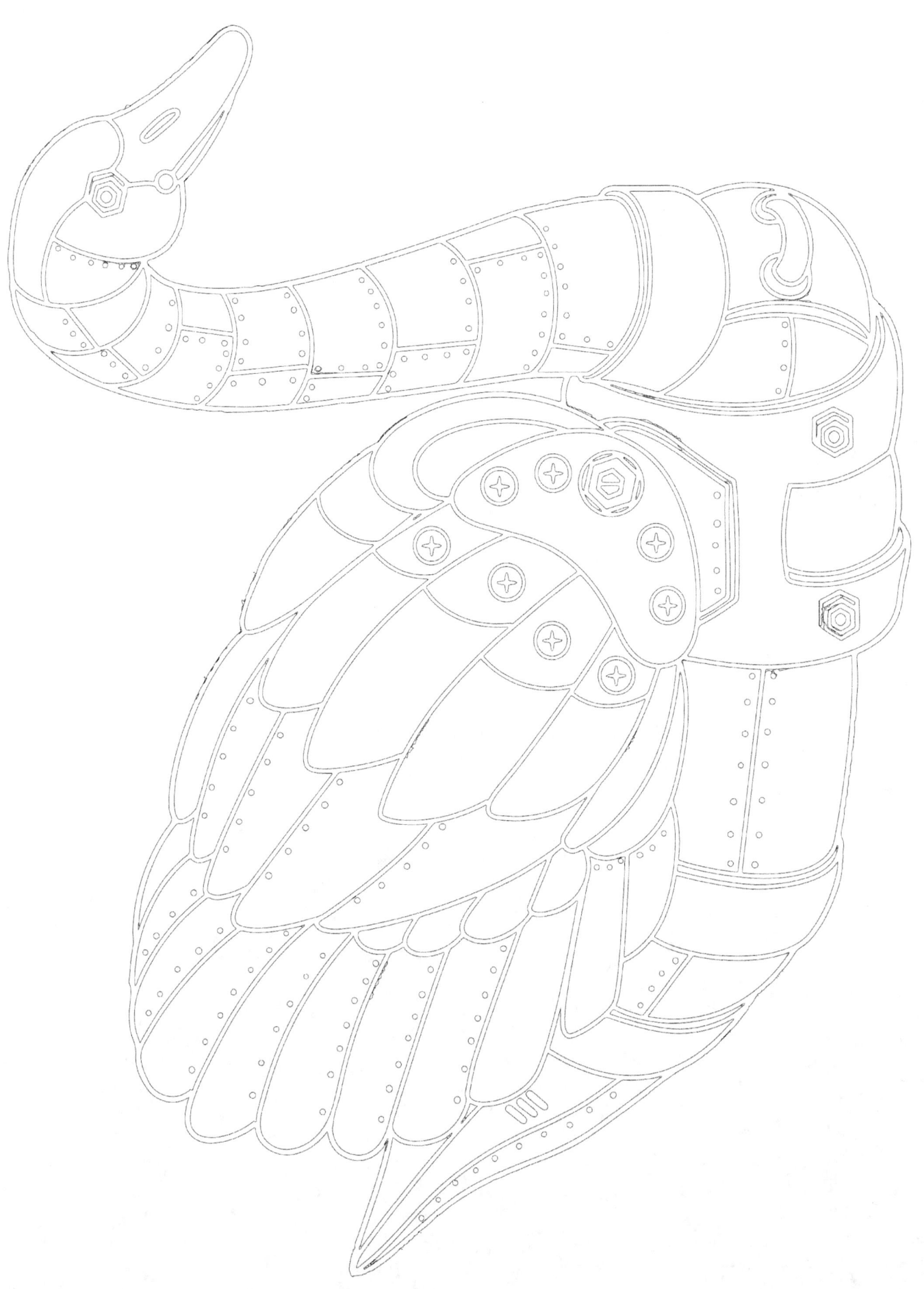

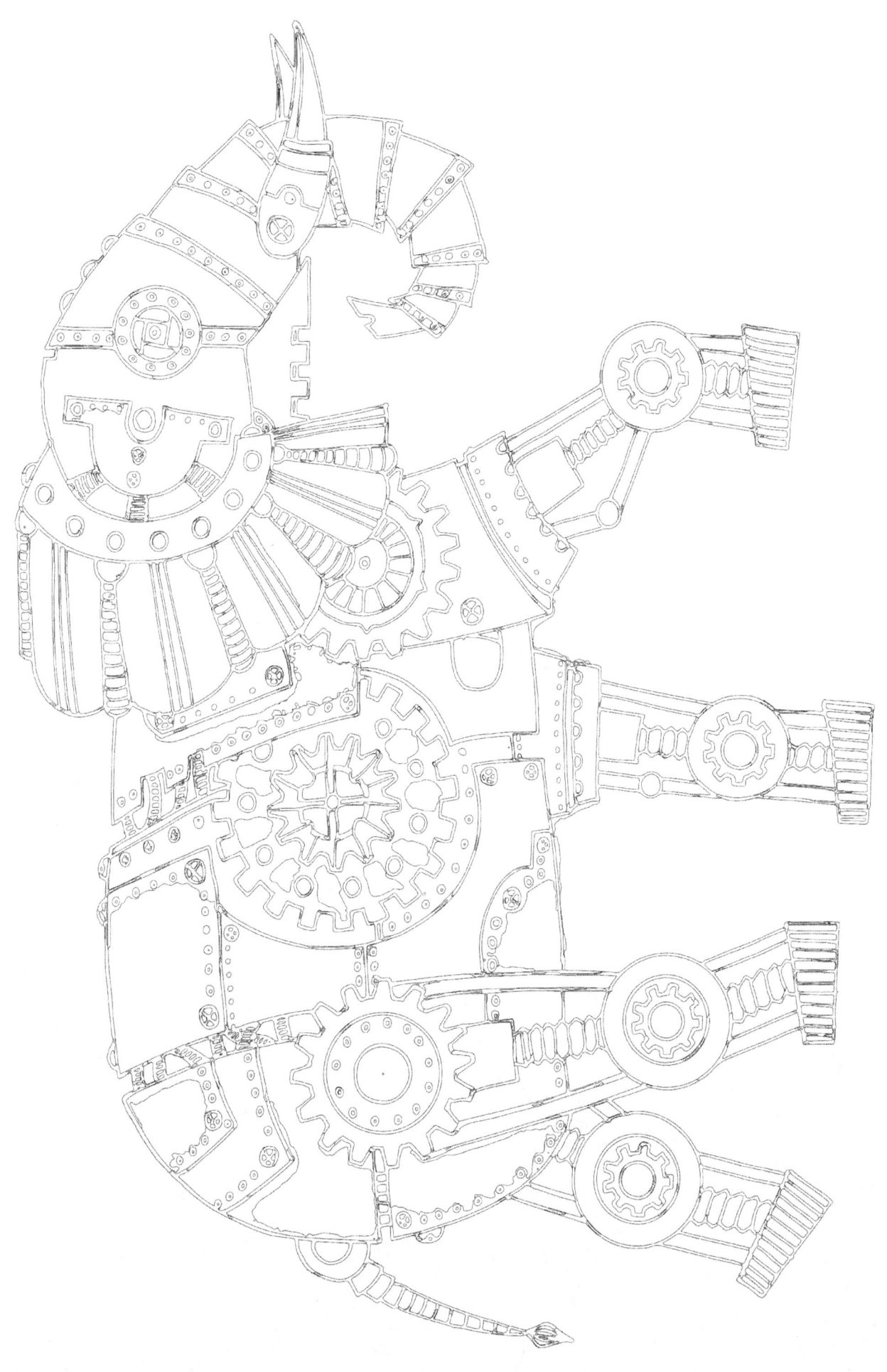

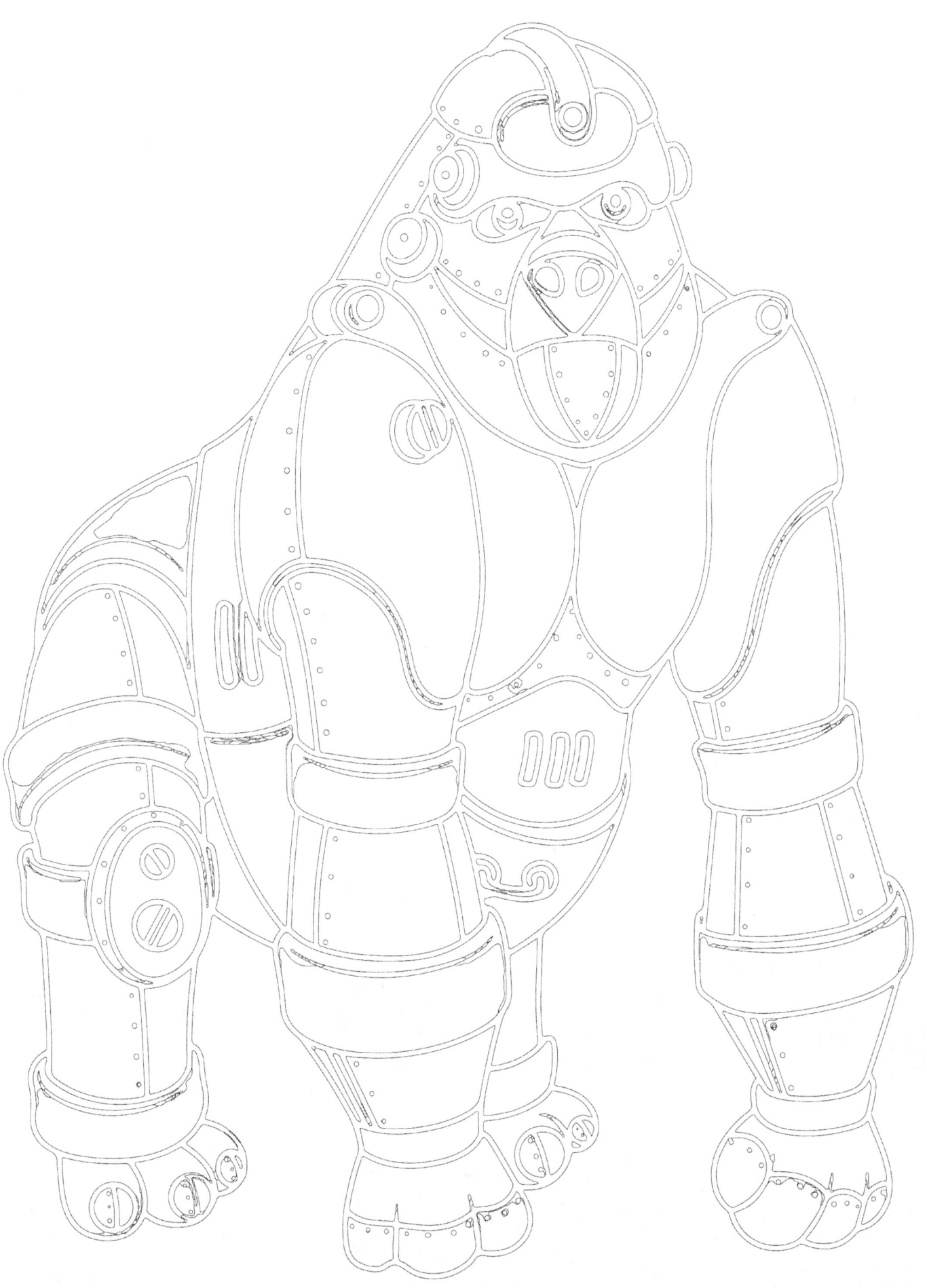

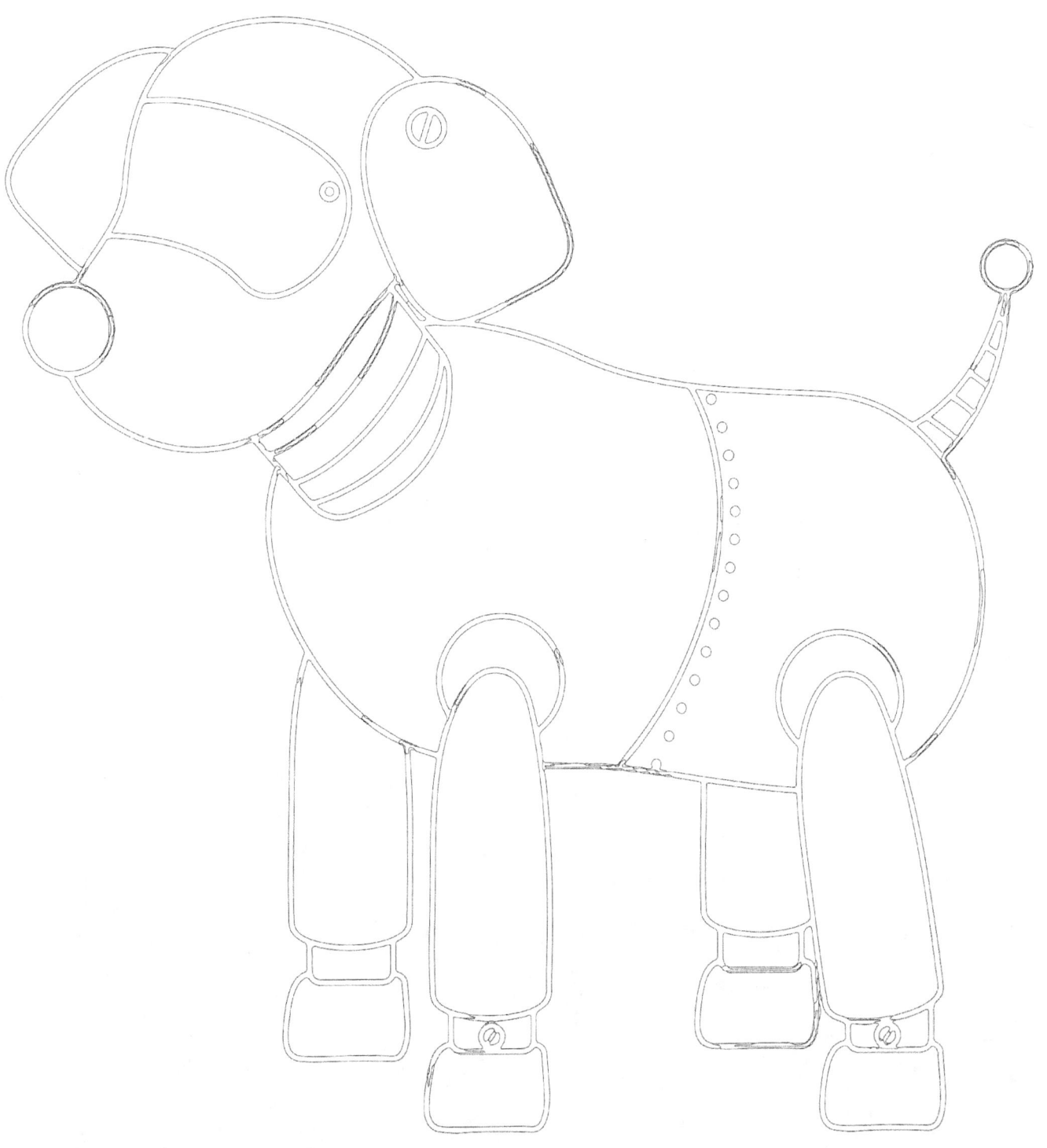

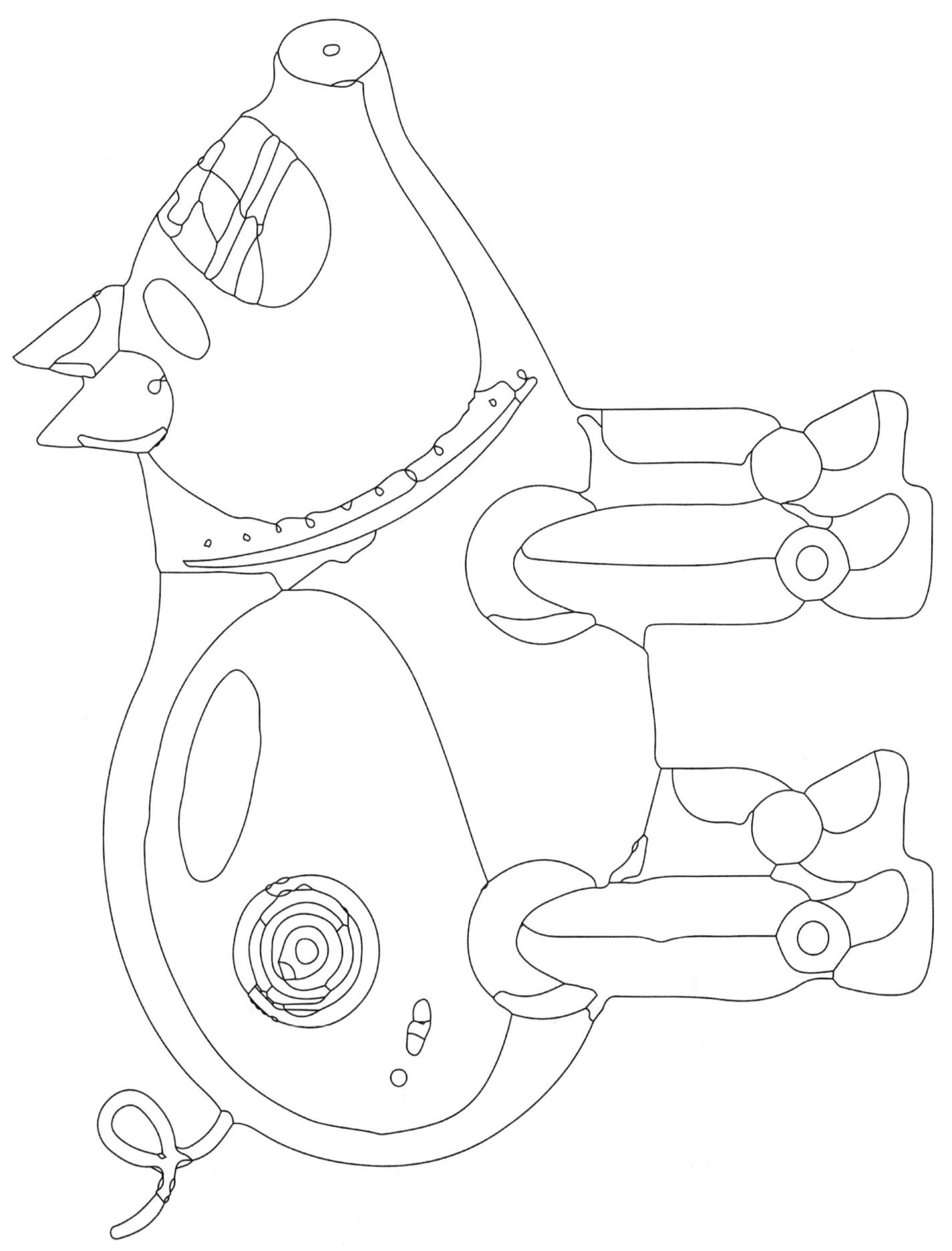

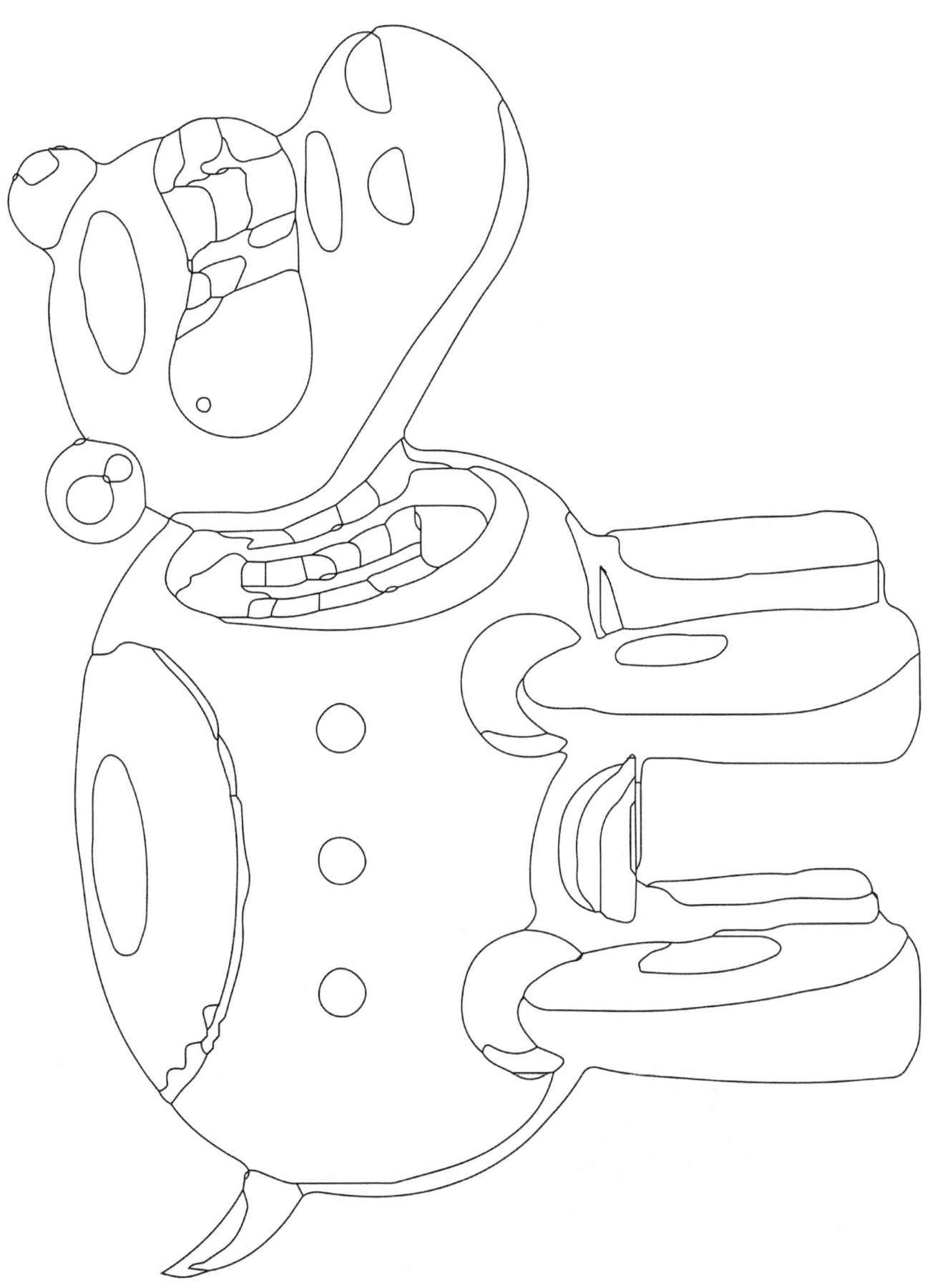

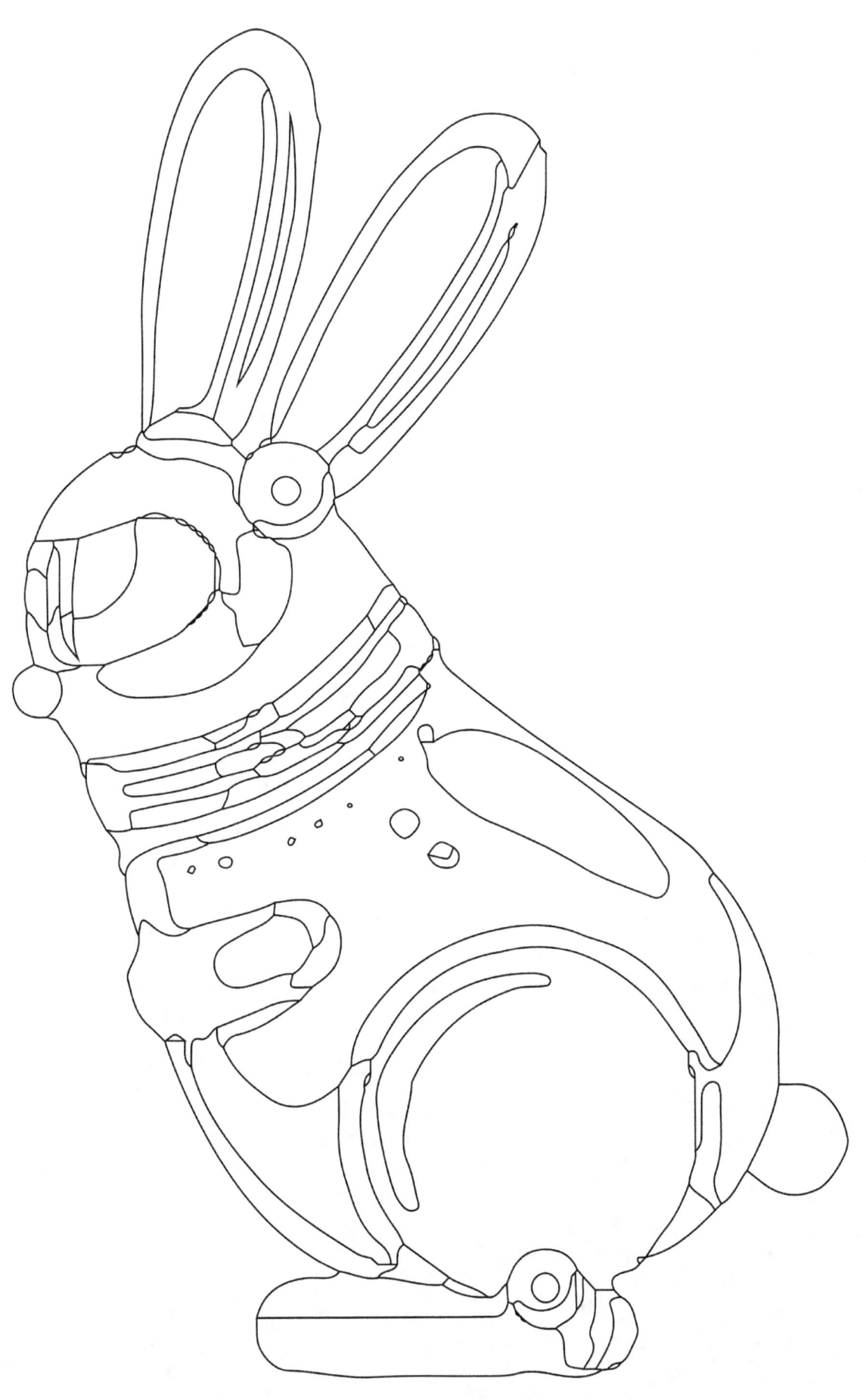

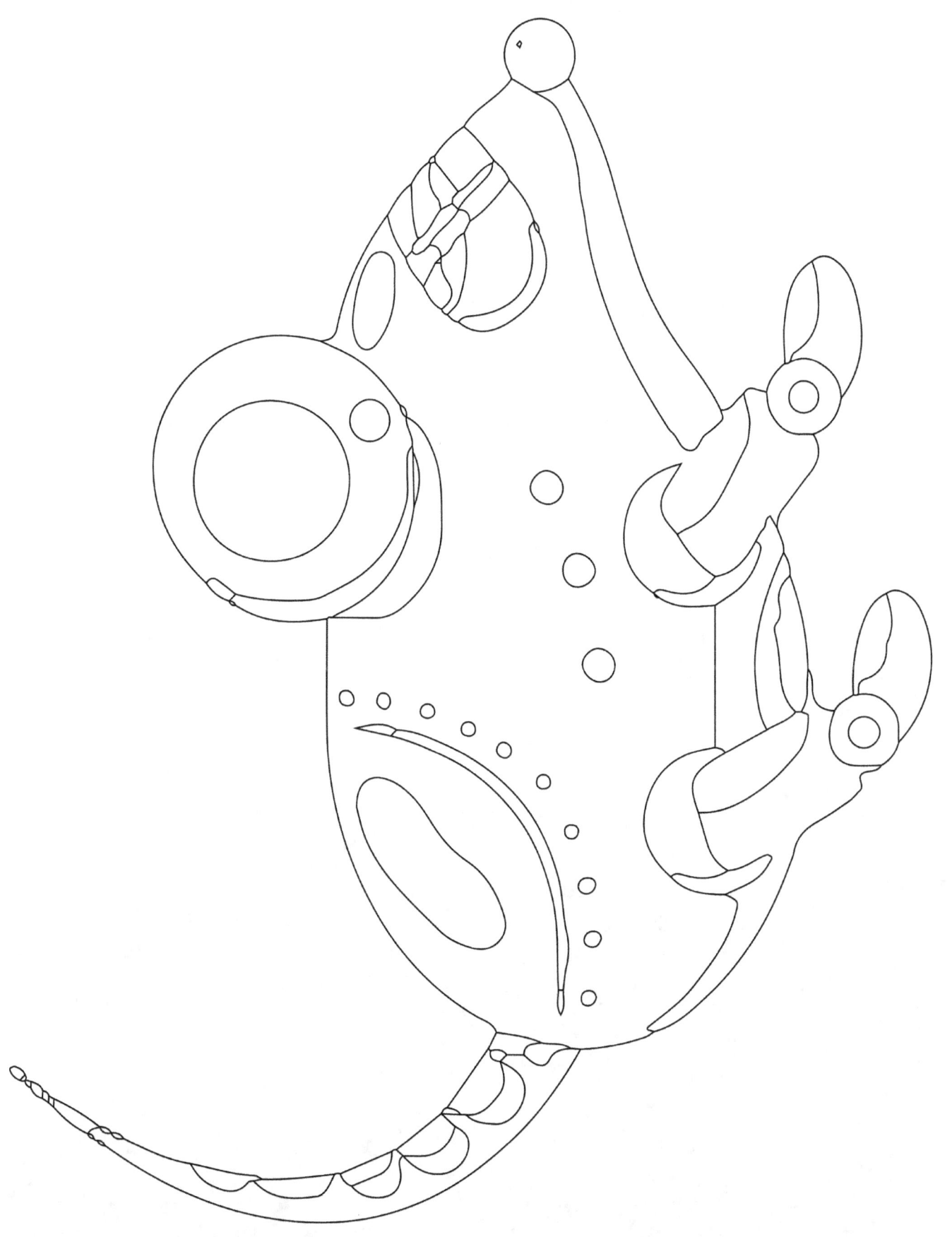

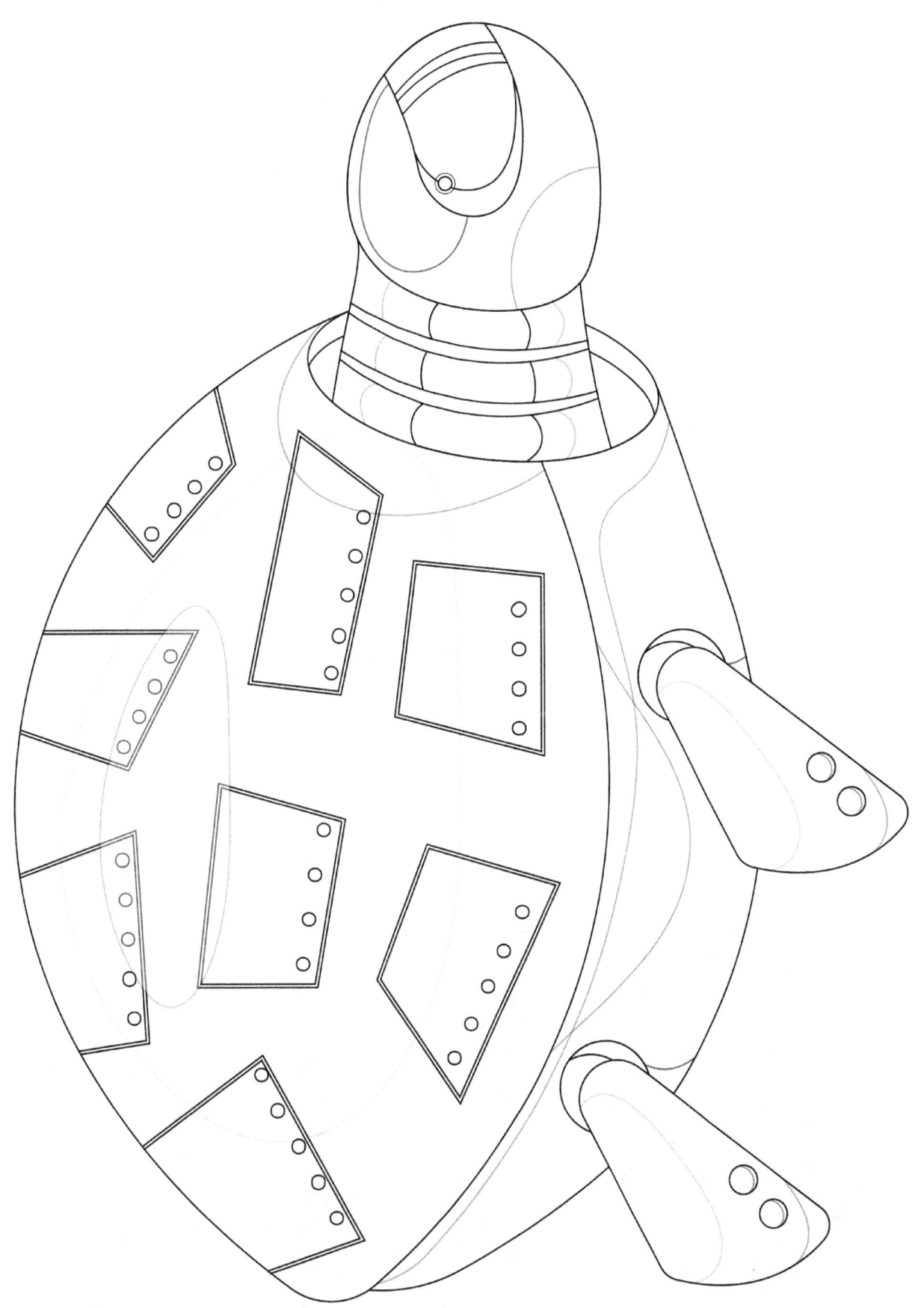

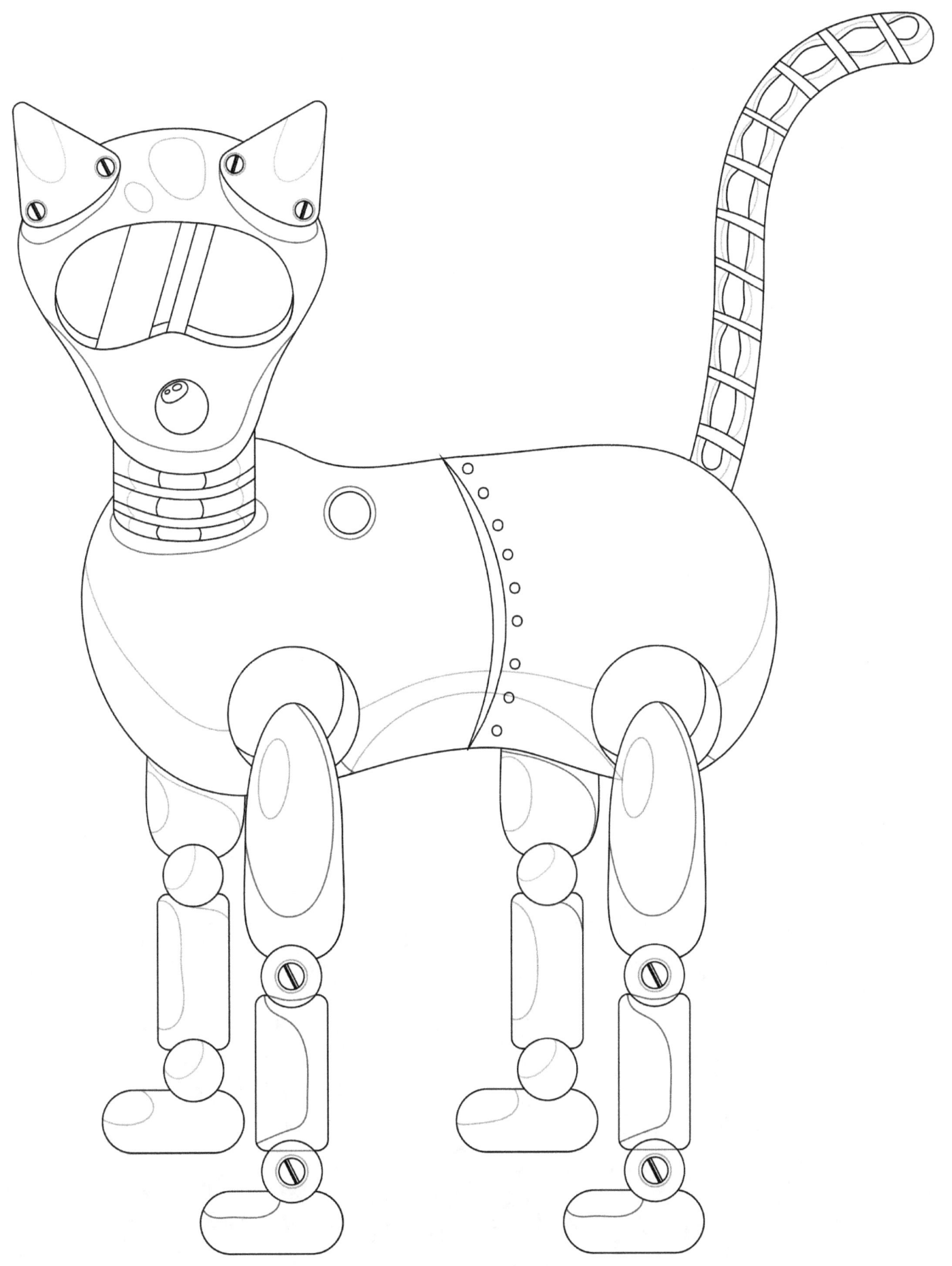

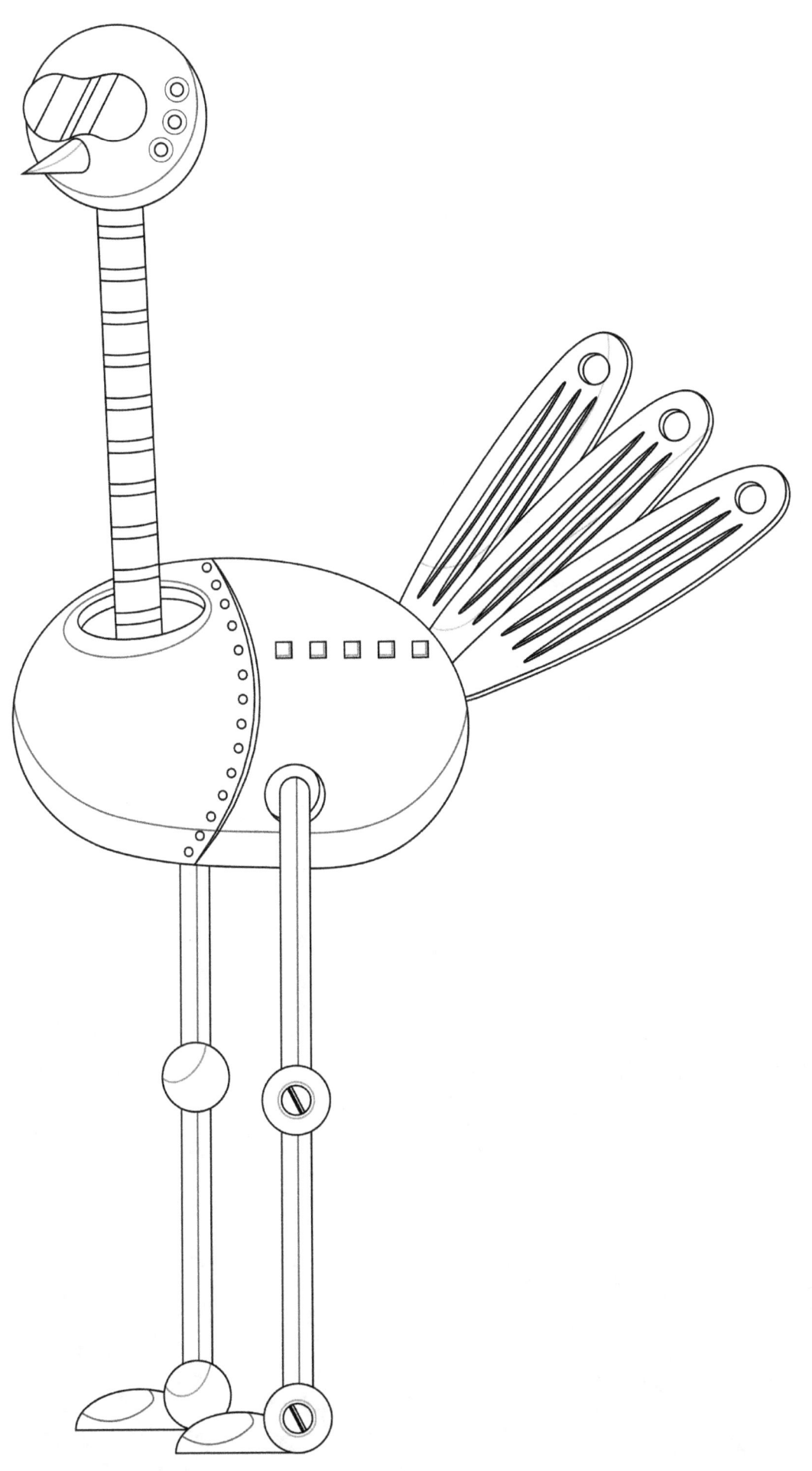

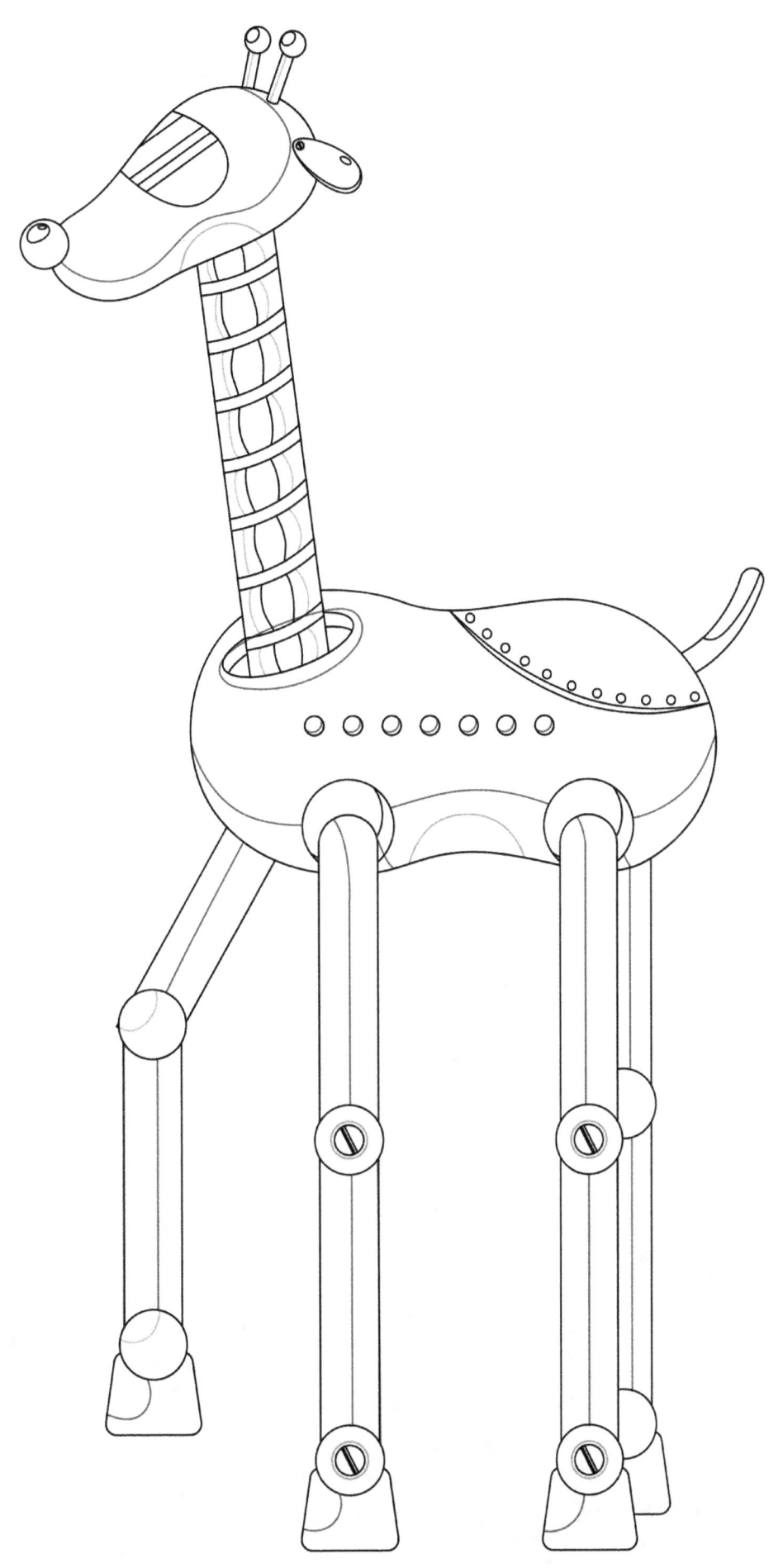

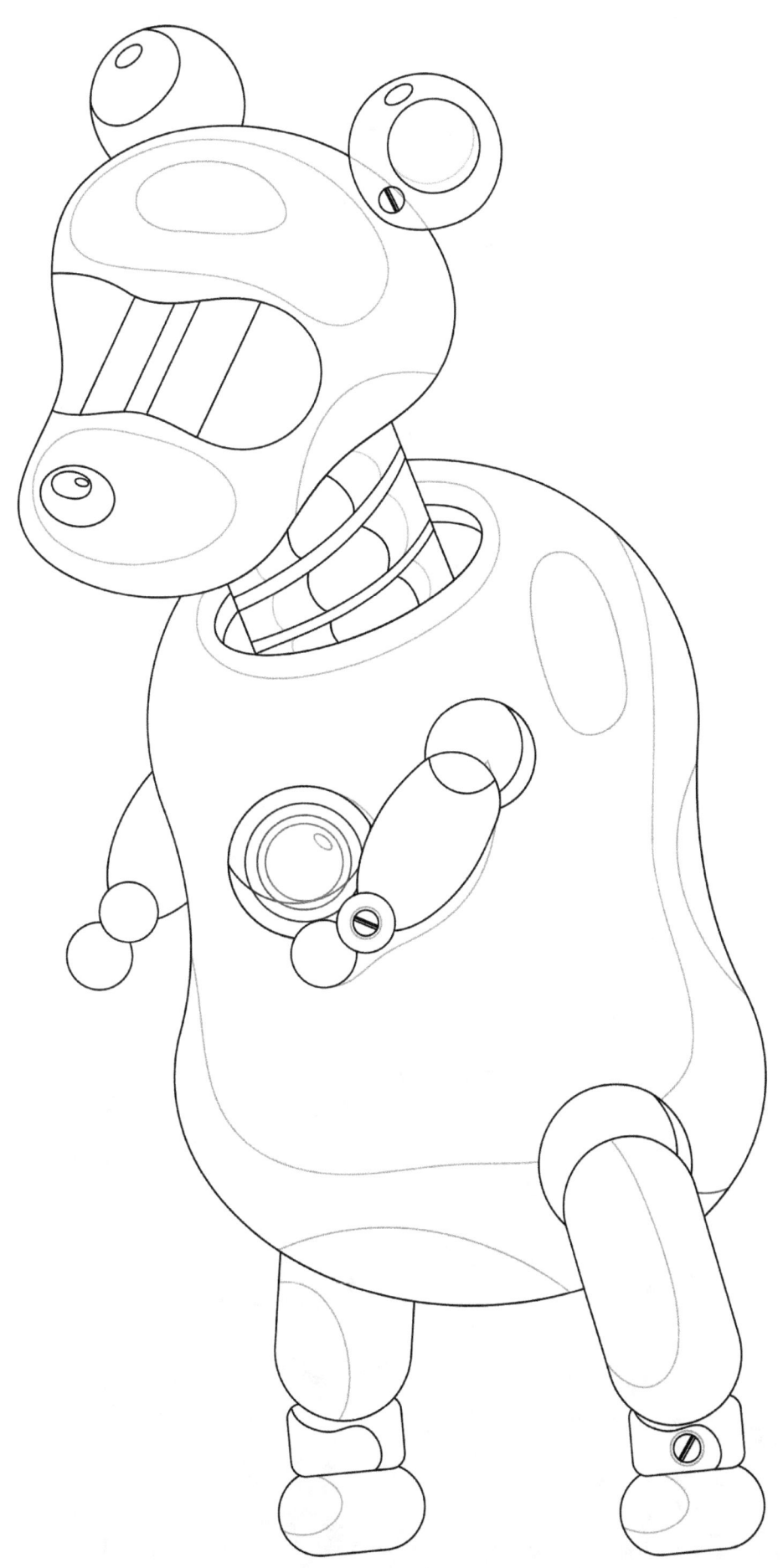

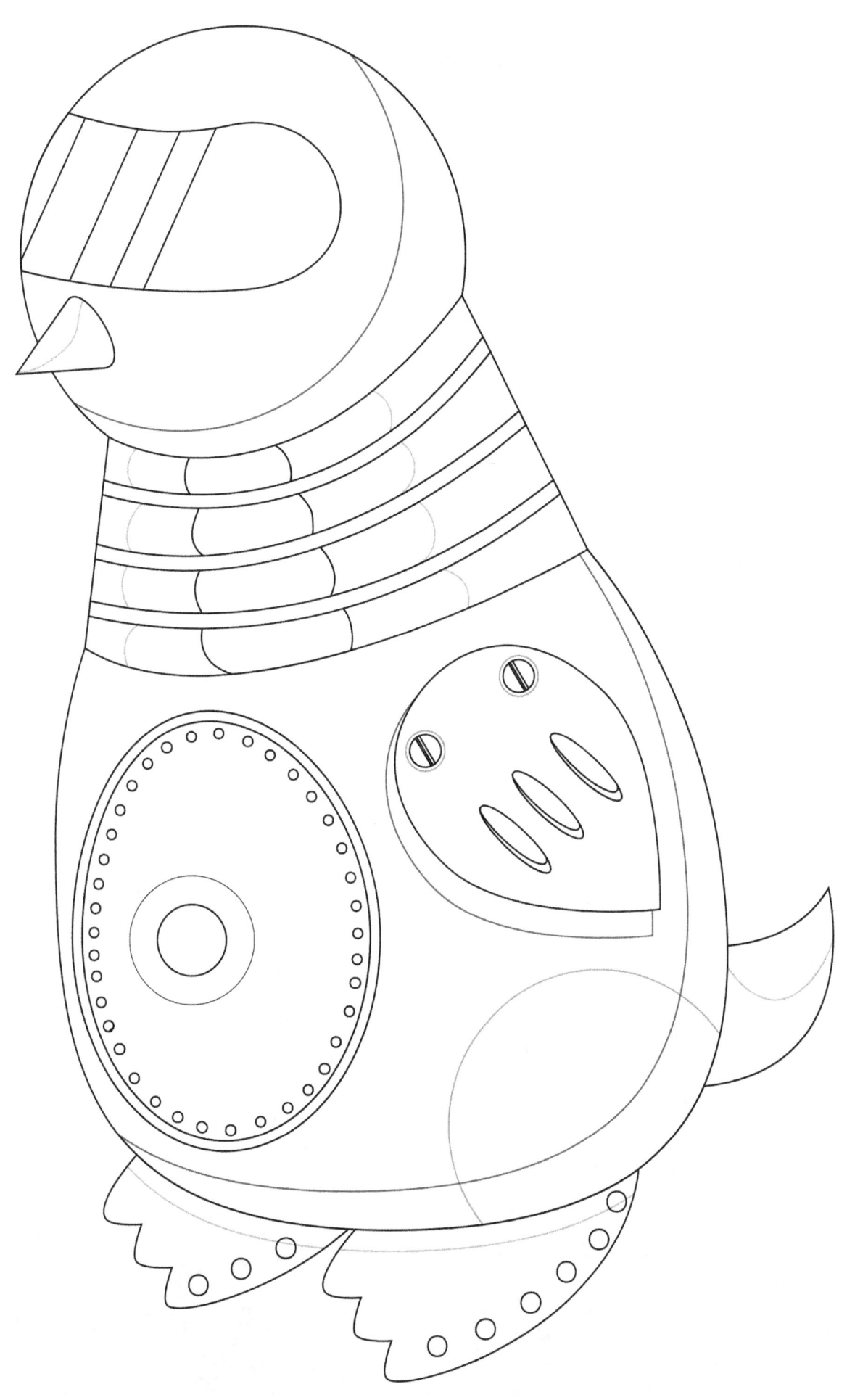

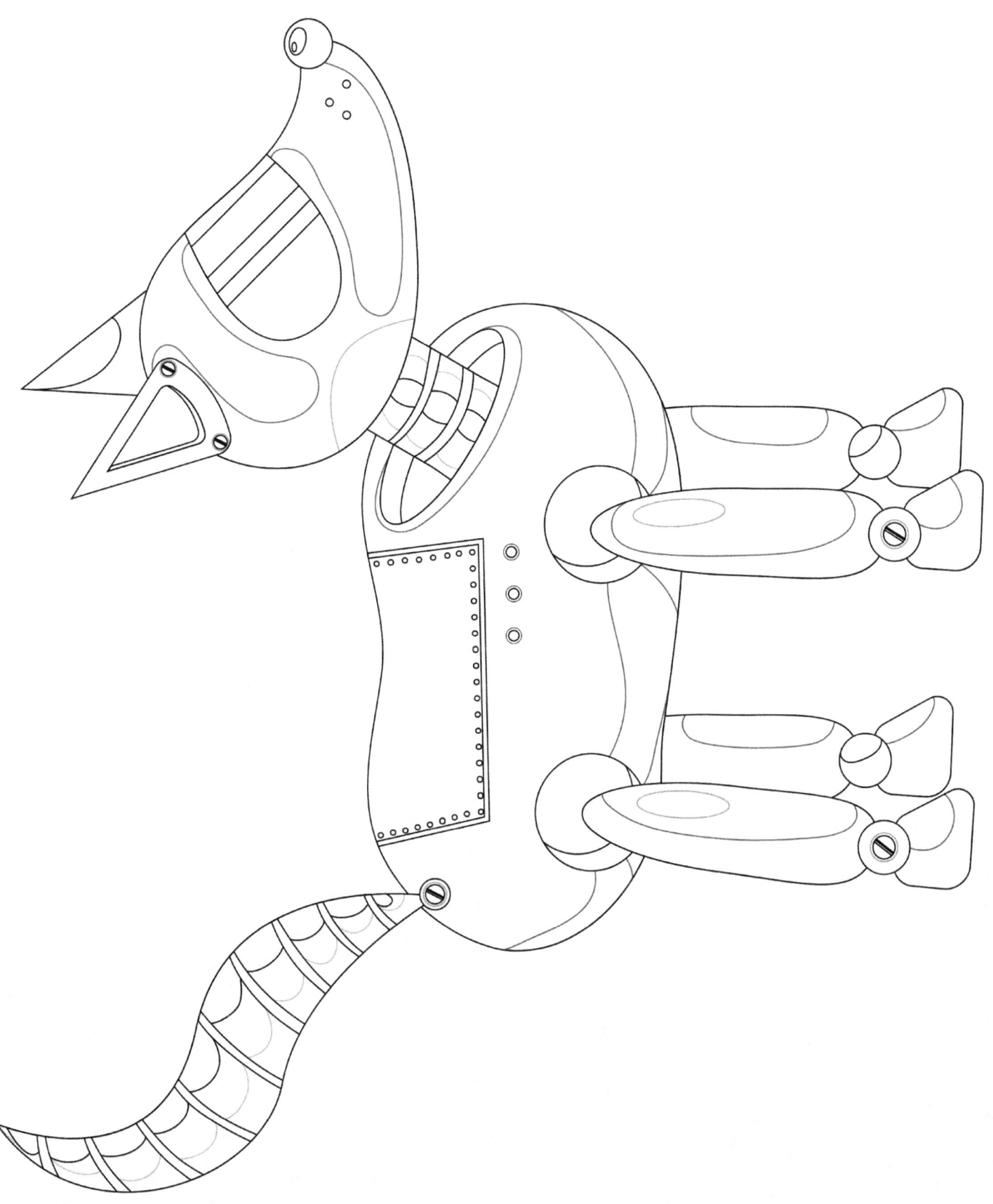

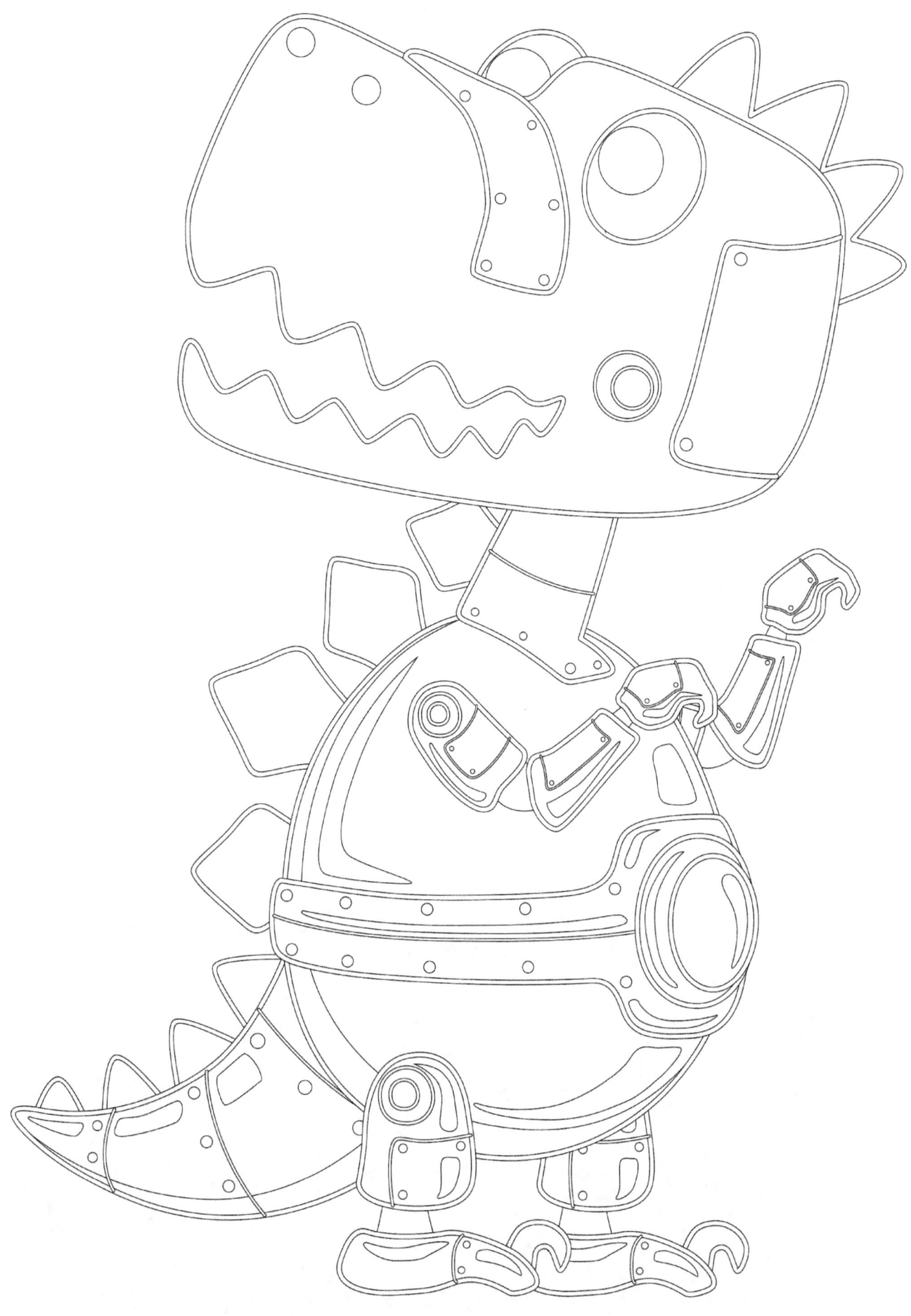

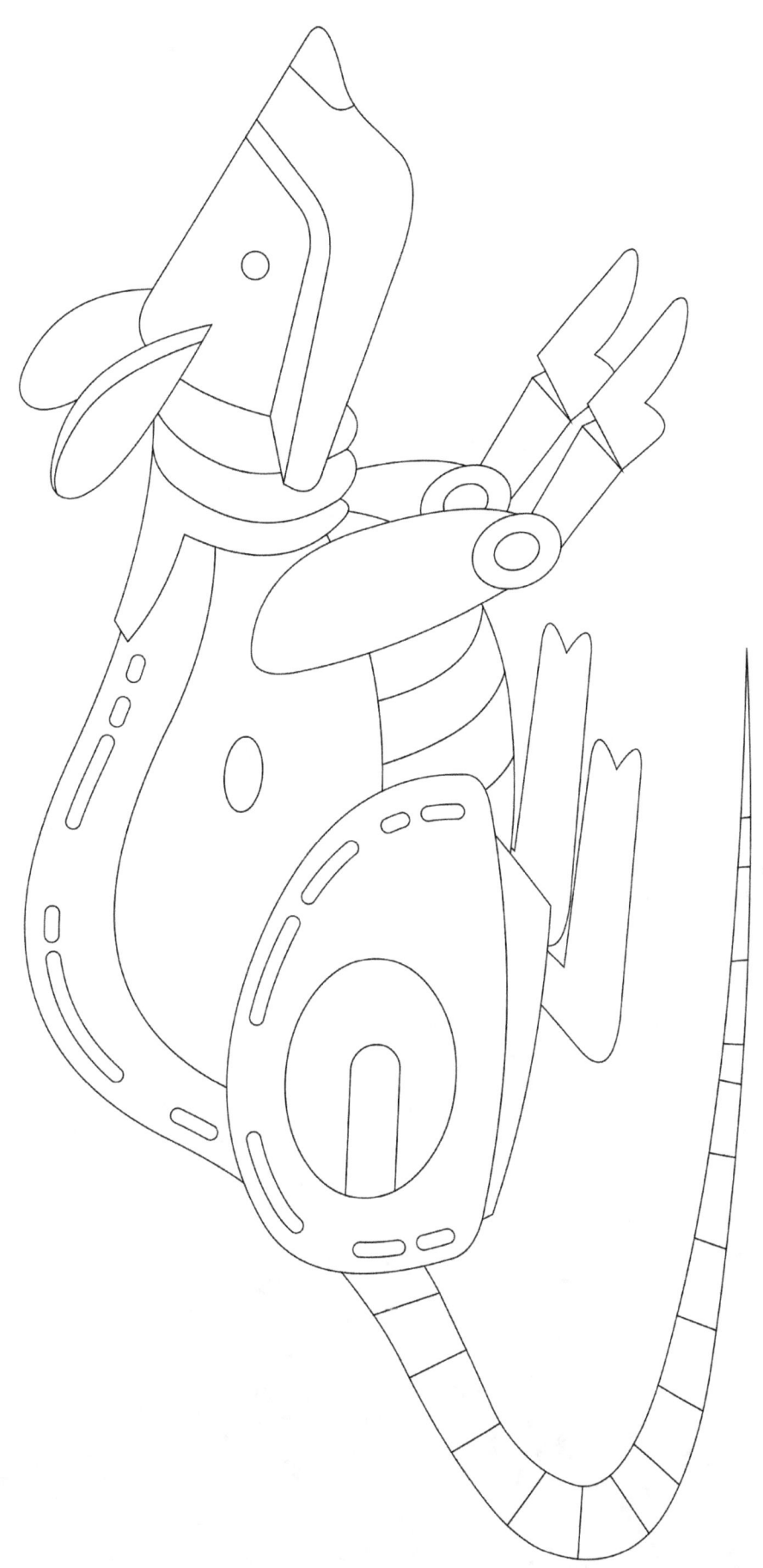

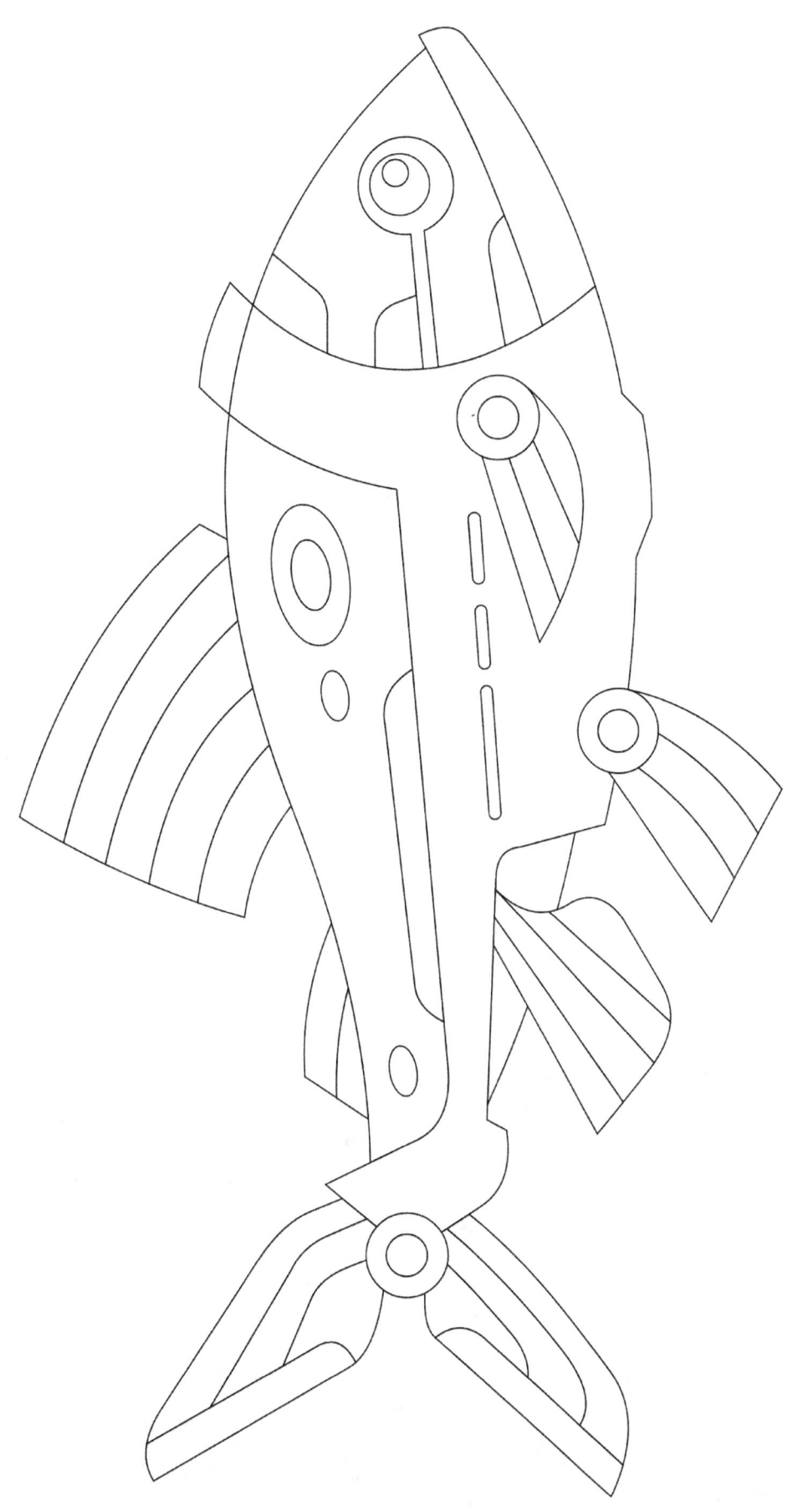

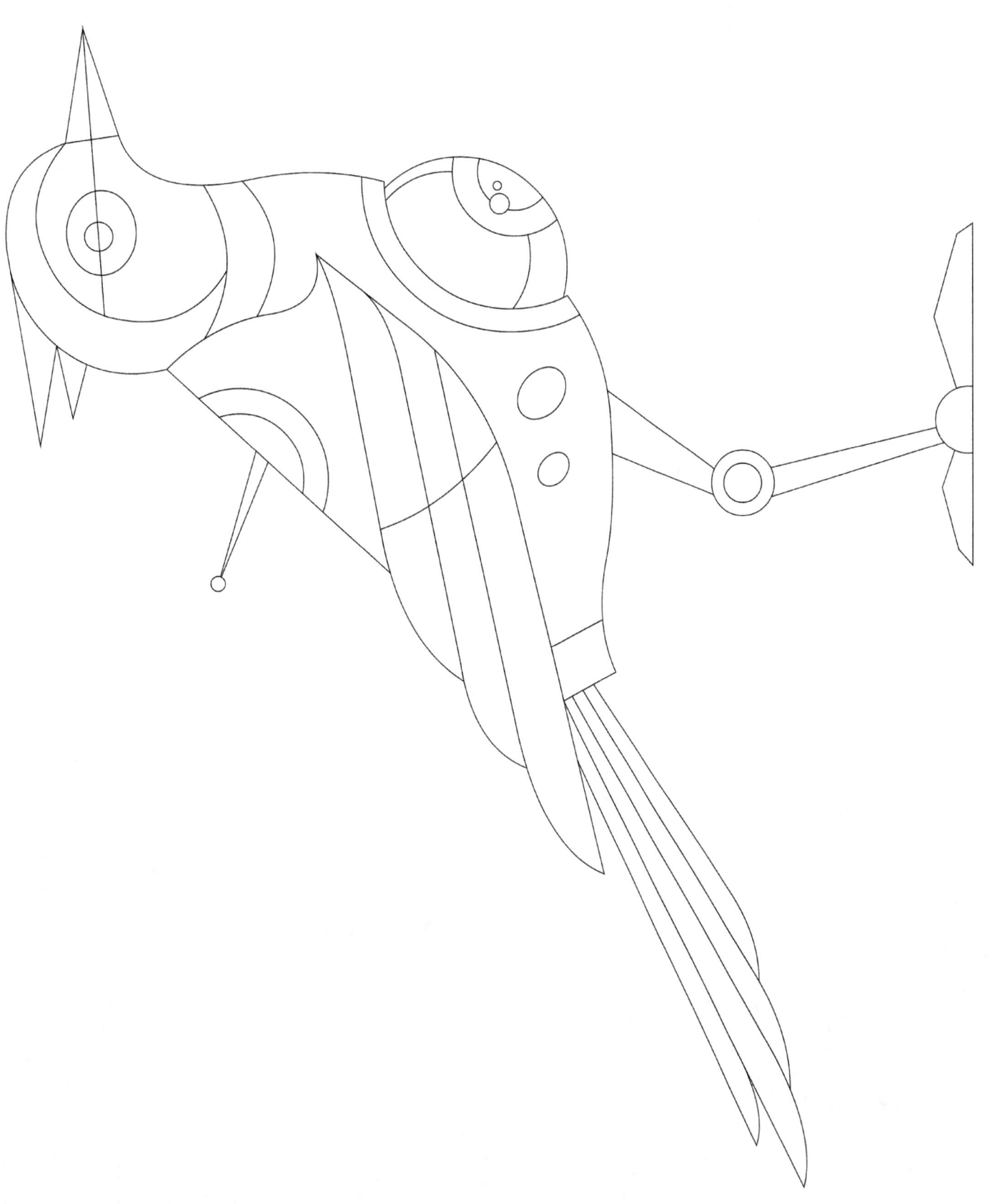

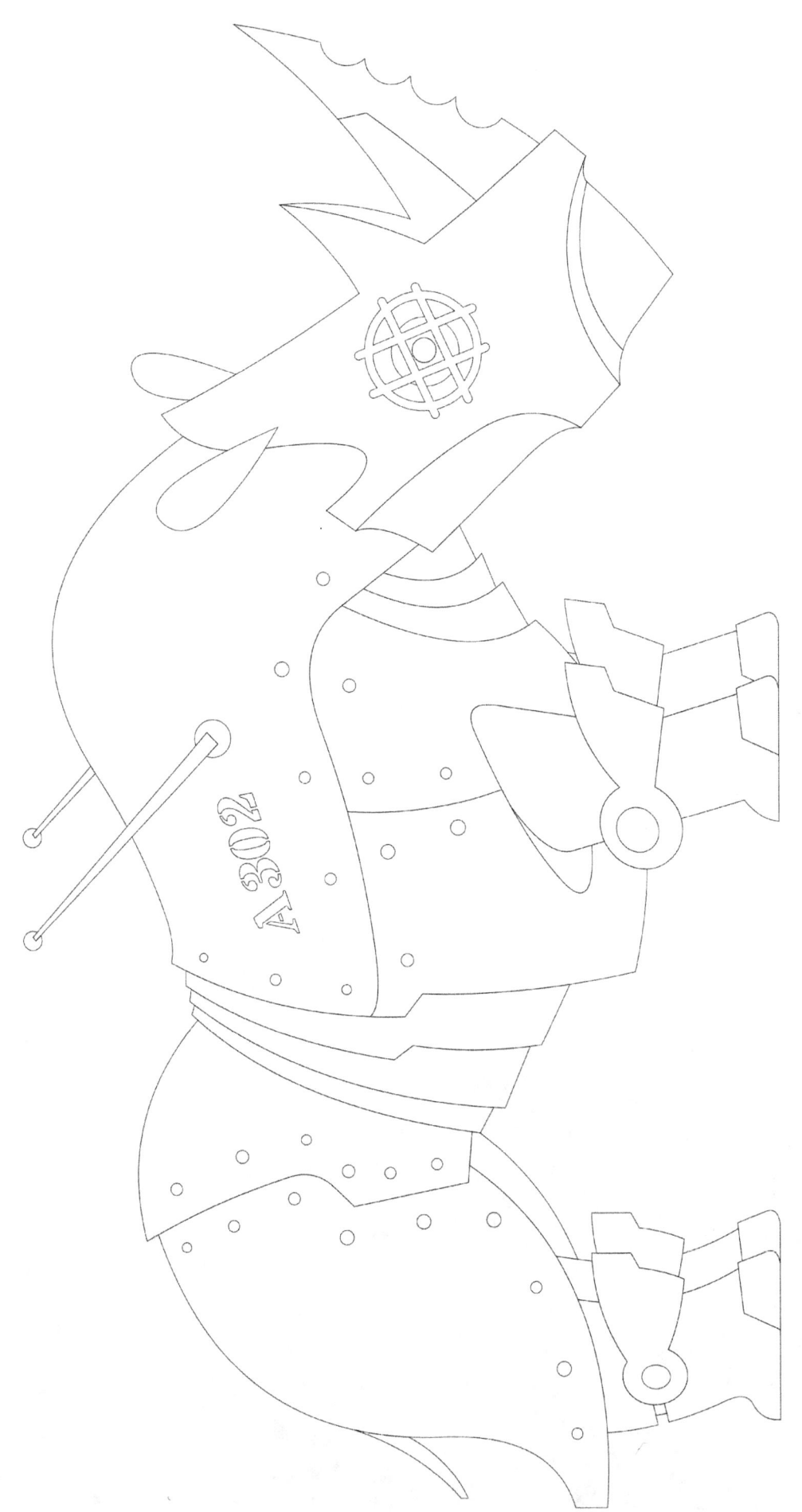

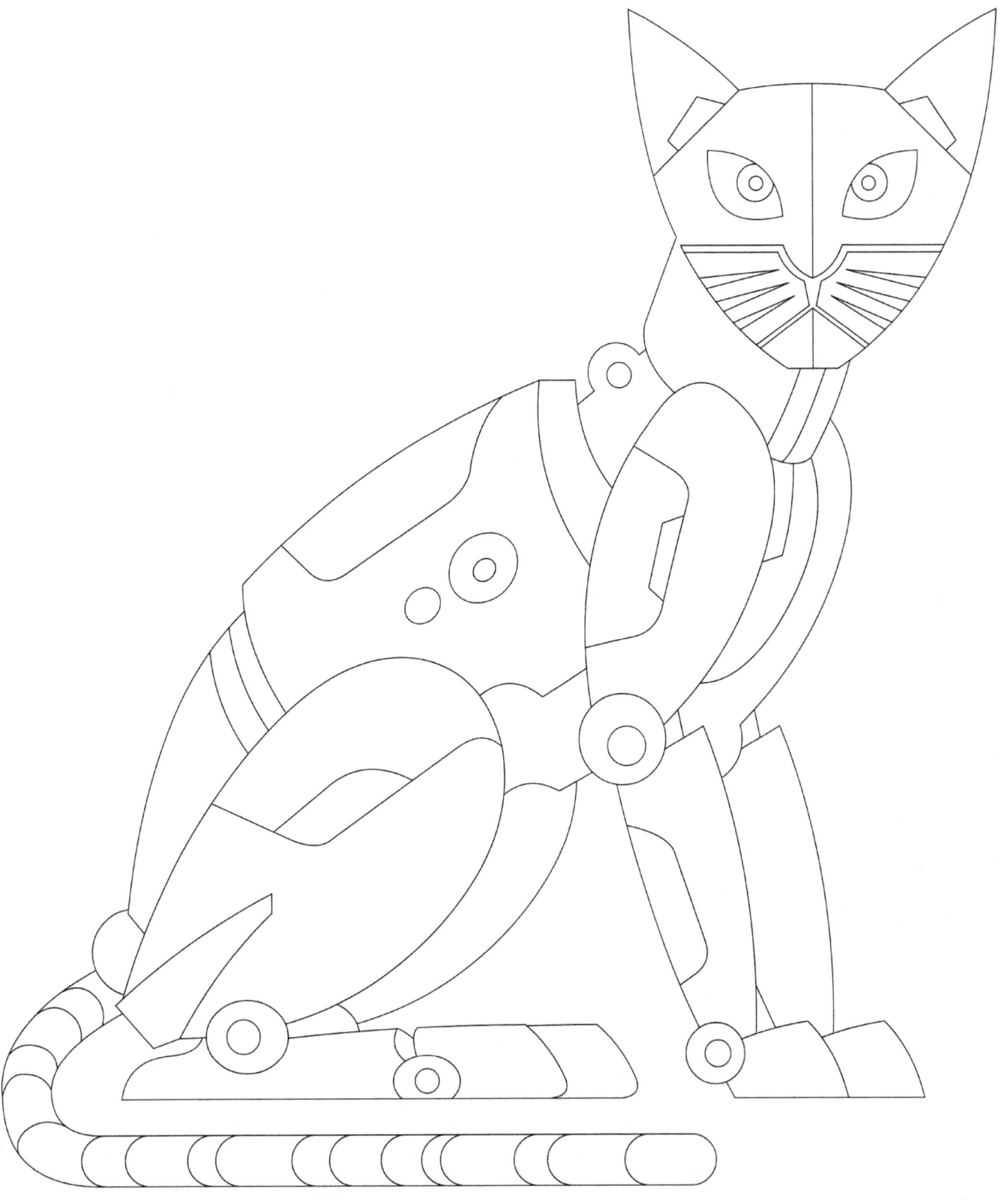

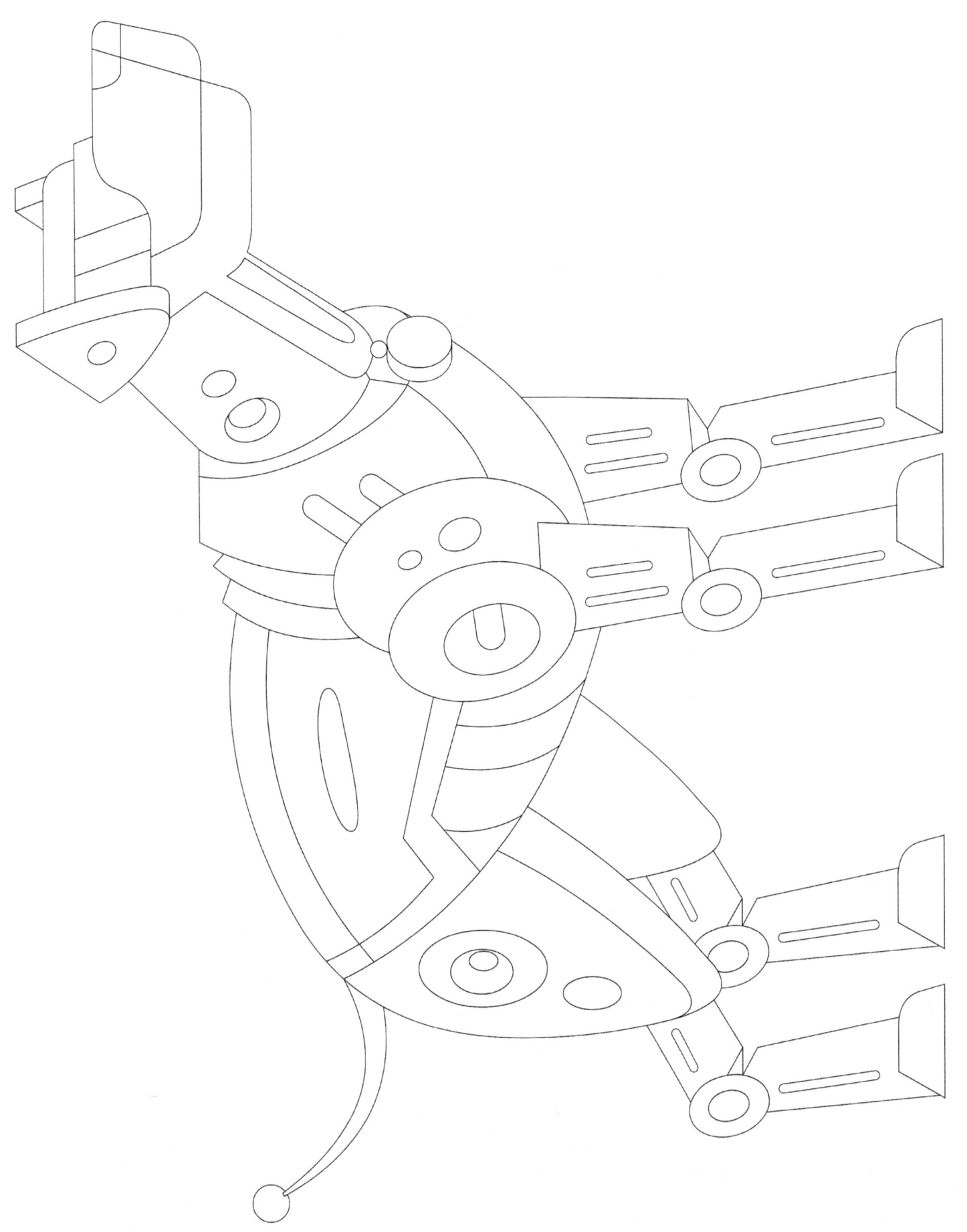

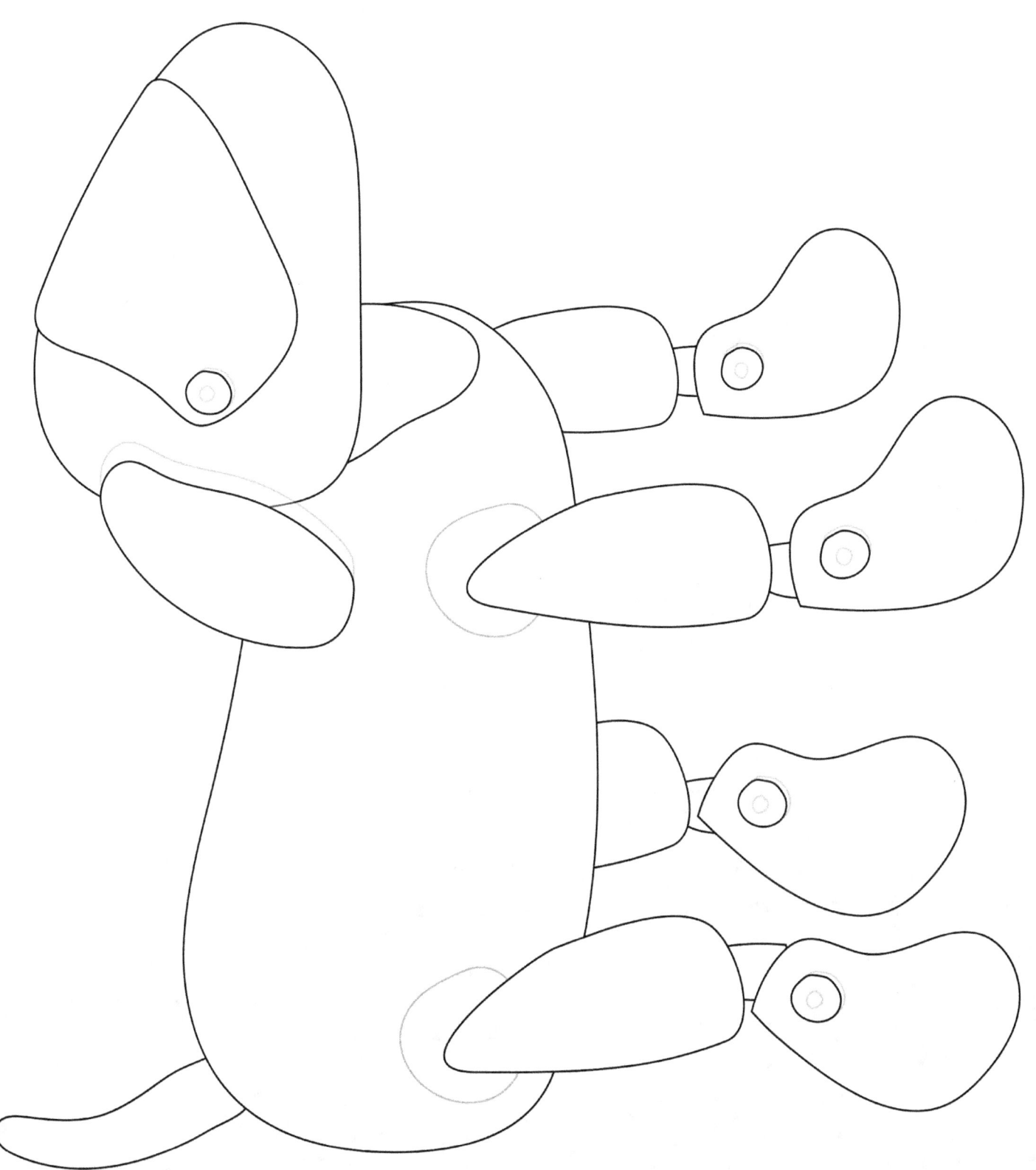

www.ingramcontent.com/pod-product-compliance
Lightning Source LLC
Chambersburg PA
CBHW080512220526
45465CB00006B/2454